DEVELOPING UNRELENTING DRIVE, DEDICATION, AND DETERMINATION

Distinct from other success or motivation books that emphasize skills, tactics, or pop gimmicks, *Developing Unrelenting Drive, Dedication, and Determination* digs deep into the theory and practice of Rational Emotive Behavior Therapy (REBT) to grow those qualities of character and personality that drive one to relentlessly do what is necessary to produce the great results one wants in life. Each chapter begins with an engaging discussion of that chapter's theme, replete with interesting real-life examples. Then comes a detailed step-by-step workshop that contains guided exercises that aid readers in building that character trait in others or themselves. Provided next are three powerful intensifiers to strengthen and integrate the trait into one's character structure. Following that are cogent suggestions to integrate that chapter's character trait into an organization's culture. Last, suggested readings are provided for those interested in further pursuing the building of that trait. *Developing Unrelenting Drive, Dedication, and Determination* is designed to instruct helping professionals in the REBT approach, to be a resource to work collaboratively with their patients or clients, and to be a sourcebook for the interested layperson.

Russell Grieger, PhD, is a licensed clinical psychologist with more than 35 years' experience of treating individuals, couples, and families, an organizational consultant to hundreds of companies, agencies, and service groups, and an adjunct professor at the University of Virginia.

DEVELOPING UNRELENTING DRIVE, DEDICATION, AND DETERMINATION

A Cognitive Behavior Workbook

Russell Grieger, PhD

Routledge
Taylor & Francis Group

NEW YORK AND LONDON

First published 2017

by Routledge
605 Third Avenue, New York, NY 10017

and by Routledge
2 Park Square, Milton Park, Abingdon, Oxon, OX14 4RN

Routledge is an imprint of the Taylor & Francis Group, an informa business

Library of Congress Cataloging-in-Publication Data
Names: Grieger, Russell, author.
Title: Developing unrelenting drive, dedication, and determination: a cognitive behavior workbook / by Russell Grieger, PhD.
Description: New York, NY: Routledge, 2017. | Includes bibliographical references and index.
Identifiers: LCCN 2016030686| ISBN 9781138185852 (hbk : alk. paper) | ISBN 9781138185869 (pbk. : alk. paper) | ISBN 9781315644219 (ebk)
Subjects: LCSH: Rational emotive behavior therapy.
Classification: LCC RC489.R3 G73 2017 | DDC 616.89/14—dc23
LC record available at https://lccn.loc.gov/2016030686

ISBN: 978-1-138-18585-2 (hbk)
ISBN: 978-1-138-18586-9 (pbk)
ISBN: 978-1-315-64421-9 (ebk)

Typeset in Dante
by Keystroke, Neville Lodge, Tettenhall, Wolverhampton

With deep love and undying appreciation
to my mother,
Florence Lillian Grieger,
and to my father,
Russell Marvin Grieger

I don't believe that God put us on earth to be ordinary.
Lou Holtz

Contents

CHAPTER 1

The Unrelenting Drive, Dedication, and Determination Factor

Great results are always within
our grasp – but what does it take?

People sometimes attribute my success to my genius;
all the genius I know anything about is hard work.
Alexander Hamilton

Let me welcome you to *Developing Unrelenting Drive, Dedication, and Determination: A Cognitive Behavior Workbook.* I wrote this book for three audiences:

1. for my coaching, consulting, and clinical colleagues who want to add cognitive behavior strategies to their arsenal in helping their clients achieve the extraordinary results they want and deserve;
2. for individuals and groups to use in collaboration with their coach, consultant, or clinician in developing what it takes to sustain high effort and productivity;
3. for those individuals and groups who want to work on their own to build the drive necessary to achieve their treasured goals.

Now, why did I write this book? Simple. For over 35 years, as a clinical psychologist, an organizational consultant, and a positive psychology growth coach, I have been sought out to help people achieve something of high value. I believe I've been quite helpful in most of these cases. But, alas, I have sometimes bumped up against clients who, despite my best efforts, would simply not step forward and work with me to get to the promised land.

I think of Will, one of my clinical clients, who, despite the piercing pain of a severe anxiety disorder, refused to follow through with the between-session therapy assignments that would have brought him blessed relief. Then there was the major Midwestern bank that hired me to help shore up their leadership team's abysmally low morale. Despite the spirited conversations that generated high-quality action strategies, their follow-through proved perfunctory and their performance continued on a slow, downtrending glide path. Finally, consider the

CEO who asked me to coach him to be more positive with his management team, only to float along in his same old negative patterns when in the thick of things.

I tried everything I could think of to get these people to act. I saw to it that they learned the necessary skills. I worked to build up their confidence. I cajoled, reasoned, provided rewards and punishments, did cost/benefit analyses, even pleaded, all in an attempt to increase their motivation. Sometimes I felt I worked harder on their behalf than they themselves did.

Finally, after similar long and hard struggles with other recalcitrant clients, breaking through with some, failing with others, I knew I had to take a step back and rethink what I was doing. Through this process, I discovered three truths that hit me with more clarity than I'd ever had about anything before:

1. To produce any desired result – be it concrete (e.g., completing a novel, getting the lawn mowed, building a financial nest egg) or something less tangible (e.g., personal happiness, marital harmony, physical health) – is actually quite simple. A person must do whatever it takes to produce that result. Visioning won't make it happen. Wanting and hoping certainly won't. Even being motivated, in and of itself, won't do the job. The only thing that will produce a desired result is for a person to act in such a way that the result is produced – no matter how long it takes, how difficult it may be, how many obstacles there may be in the path.

2. Sounds simple, doesn't it? But, I came to realize that, no matter what the desired result may be, nobody is capable of sustaining motivation 100% of the time. In other words, no matter how prized the result one wants, a person will be highly motivated to achieve it at times, but not so at others. Some people simply tire out. Others don't really care that much to begin with. Still others are blocked by psychological forces stronger than their enthusiasm. Suffice it to say that, as a by-product of the vagaries of human existence, people's enthusiasm for anything will wax and wane over time, as thusly will their efforts and hence their results.

    No wonder my attempts to motivate my unmotivated clients failed. Like so many others, I had viewed motivation as an emotional phenomenon. I fell into the trap of trying to inspire them to be more aroused, caring, and excited to reach their goals. Like an athletic coach, I tried to fire these people up, arouse their passion, spur them to leave their blood on the field. But, these were the exact inner states that naturally rise and fall in all human beings over time.

3. Given this, I figured that, if I were to help my unmotivated clients relentlessly act to achieve their valued goals, I'd have to find a new approach to motivation. I'd have to discover the key to sustained action even when one is unmotivated. *Motivation without motivation*, I thought, *that's a hell of a concept.*

These three truths, then, gave birth to *Developing Unrelenting Drive, Dedication, and Determination*. I asked: How can I get my clients to sustain the necessary action to produce their valued results, whether motivated or not? What does it take to do so, no matter what the intended result, the prevailing circumstances, or the feeling state? What is it that, once developed, will spur a person to relentlessly act, no matter how he or she feels?

Fortunately, the answers to these questions were available. Hundreds of research studies from all over the world provided the pathways. They are three in number and they are layered. Here they are.

THE HOW: HARD WORK AND DELIBERATE PRACTICE

Miracles sometimes occur, but one has to work terribly hard for them.
Chaim Weizmann

The most common explanation for why a certain few create great results is that they are blessed with some special talent or skill. Beethoven was born a genius, as was Thomas Jefferson, Sir Isaac Newton, and Bob Dylan. Despite this prevalent perception, Geoff Colvin, in his provocative 2008 book *Talent is Overrated: What Really Separates World-Class Performers from Everybody Else*, shares a vast body of literature across a wide array of fields that proves that this simply is not so. It seems that the idea that some people are born a world-class musician, salesperson, or athlete is a myth.

Indeed, Colvin's research shows that what distinguishes people who achieve extraordinary results is what he calls "deliberate practice." In addition to just plain old hard work, deliberate practice is characterized by several features:

1. It is an activity specifically designed to improve a particular performance.
2. It can be repeated over and over.
3. There is an opportunity for continuous feedback from a teacher, coach, or mentor.
4. It requires a high degree of focus and concentration.
5. It is not necessarily enjoyable or fun.
6. The earlier in life one begins to practice and the more one does it, the more likely one will be great at it.

Malcolm Gladwell, the author of *Outliers: The Story of Success* (2008), tells us that experts have concluded that 10,000 hours of such practice is required for true excellence. He quotes the noted neurologist Daniel Levitin, who writes:

The emerging picture from such studies is that ten thousand hours of practice is required to achieve the level of mastery associated with being a world-class expert – in anything. In study after study of composers, basketball players, fiction writers, ice skaters, concert pianists, chess players, master criminals, and what have you, this number comes up again and again. It seems that it takes the brain this long to assimilate all that it needs to know to achieve true mastery. (p. 40)

To put flesh and blood to this, let's take a brief look at three notables who most of us would agree achieved great things in some valued area of their lives:

- **The Beatles.** The Beatles burst into international fame seemingly overnight. Generally thought to be the best rock 'n' roll band ever, they conquered America in 1964 with such appealing ditties as "Love Me Do," "Please Please Me," and "I Want to Hold Your Hand." But, guess what? They labored in obscurity for seven full years, beginning in 1957 when John Lennon and Paul McCartney first met. During those seven years, The Beatles performed live an estimated 1,200 times before they famously first appeared on *The Ed Sullivan Show*. These included five trips to the red light district of Hamburg, Germany where they were expected to perform seven days a week for anywhere from five to eight hours at a time. It was a full ten years of non-stop deliberate practice from their beginnings to their masterpiece albums, *Rubber Soul*, *Sgt. Pepper's Lonely Hearts Club Band*, and *The Beatles (White Album)*.

- **Senator Ted Kennedy.** Considered to be one of the top two or three United States senators of all time, Ted Kennedy was called "the Lion of the Senate." After his memorial service on Saturday, August 29, 2009, someone asked Susan Estrich, one of the senator's former aides, whether it was his famous name or his popularity among his colleagues that was the key to his outstanding success. She acknowledged that he was well liked, even loved by those who knew him well. Yet, she went on to say that what made him such a great legislator was his ability to work longer and harder than his fellow senators.

- **Steve Martin.** Lore has it that Steve Martin burst into the national consciousness an overnight comedic genius. He first appeared on the radar in 1975 and, by, 1978, he was the busiest act in the history of stand-up comedy, drawing ecstatic crowds of up to 25,000 people in arenas across the country. What seemed like a blitzkrieg success story, though, was preceded by more than two decades of preparation. In his wonderful memoir, *Born Standing Up* (2007), Martin chronicled the many years of honing his craft until he mastered it. Describing the culmination of all this hard work and deliberate practice, he said, "The disparate elements I'd begun years before had become unified; my road experience had made me tough as steel, and I had total command of my material. But most important, I felt really, really funny" (p. 165).

To sum, there is a vast amount of scientific evidence across a wide variety of fields – sales people, athletes, inventors, musicians, and business people, to name but a few – that it is hard work and deliberate practice that distinguishes people who produce great results. This was true of The Beatles, Ted Kennedy, and Steve Martin. It seems reasonable to conclude that we can all produce the great results we want, however we define them, if only we are willing to put in the necessary work and practice.

But there has to be more than just hard work and deliberate, sustained practice. What would propel a person to devote himself or herself to such extreme practice? Given the investment one would have to make in terms of time and energy, not to mention the sacrifices with regard to family, friends, and personal pleasure, one has to wonder why one would devote so much of oneself in the pursuit of these results. Why would one persist on working so long and hard for a reward that may be months away, if not years or even decades? Read on.

THE WHAT: DEDICATION AND DETERMINATION

Genius is an infinite capacity for taking life by the scruff of the neck.
Katherine Hepburn

To delve deeper into the source of sustained effort, let's refer to what I think is one of the most important business books ever written, Jim Collins' *Good to Great* (2011). Comparing great to merely good companies, Collins discovered several distinct differences between the two, perhaps the most significant illustrated in Figure 1.1.

Great companies start with disciplined people who relentlessly keep their noses to the grindstone. They stay disciplined in their thought, meaning that they see to it that everything they do is in the service of making the company's mission and vision a reality. In other words, they do not veer off onto bunny trails. Finally comes disciplined action. Disciplined action means that the company's people, from top to bottom, persist – day after day, month after month – in acting to produce great results.

Collins emphasizes that the sequence of these elements is important. Disciplined action without disciplined thought is a "recipe for disaster" (p. 126).

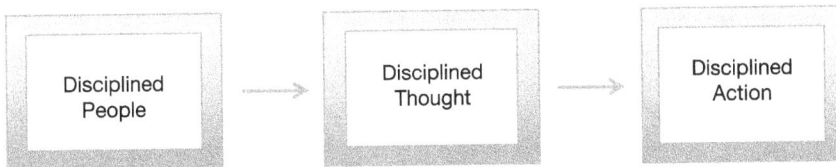

FIGURE 1.1   Elements of Great Companies

It would be like flying a jumbo jet full speed without a firm destination in mind. And disciplined thought without disciplined people is "impossible to sustain" (p. 126). So, the foundation of great companies lies with their disciplined people. Look at what Collins says about both the great companies' leaders and their employees:

- Their *leaders* are "fanatically driven, infected with an incurable need to produce sustained results. They are resolved to do whatever it takes to make the company great, no matter how big or hard the decisions" (p. 127).
- The employees "became somewhat extreme in the fulfillment of their responsibilities, bordering in some cases on fanaticism. Throughout our research, we were struck by the continual use of words like rigorous, dogged, determined, diligent, precise, fastidious, systematic, methodical, workmanlike, accountable, and responsible" (p. 127).

We intuitively know this to be true. People who work hard and produce great results almost without exception are dedicated and determined. One of my favorite quotes, of uncertain provenance but often attributed to President Calvin Coolidge, appears in *Grinding It Out* by Ray Kroc, the founding genius of the McDonald's fast food chain:

Nothing in the world can take the place of persistence. Talent will not: Nothing is more common than unsuccessful men with talent. Genius will not: Unrewarded genius is almost a proverb. Education will not: The world is full of educated derelicts. Persistence and determination alone are omnipotent. (Kroc, 1977)

So, let's summarize the how and what of extraordinary effort and results so far. From Geoff Colvin we learn that people who produce greatness are sustained hard workers. From a relatively early age, they deliberately practice their craft until they master it at a world-class level. Malcolm Gladwell tells us that the minimum number of practice hours is 10,000. This is true across a wide array of professions. And from Jim Collins we learn that the fuel that drives this type of sustained effort is self-discipline: an inner dedication and determination that is palpable.

But, as useful as all this is, we are still left with the $64,000 question: What is the source of this dedication and determination? What causes a person to bring such dedication to their efforts for such a sustained time until they bring about great results? What propels this dogged determination? As helpful as they have been, neither Colvin, Gladwell, nor Collins supply us with an explanation. We need to get to the root of these questions in order to purposely create the great life we want and deserve.

THE WHY: CHARACTER

One must be something, in order to do something.
Goethe

From my 35 years' experience of counseling, consulting, and coaching, I have come to understand that the answer to the questions posed above can be found in what I call the Tree of Extraordinary Performance and Results. As illustrated in Figure 1.2, the top of the tree, where the fruit grows, represents the Results one wants. These can be big or small, private or public, and within whatever arena that is important to a person: business, finance, marriage, parenting, friendship, physical health, emotional well-being, spirituality, or whatever.

The Means of producing great results are at the tree's trunk. They are the skills one needs in order to get the job done. These may be personal, interpersonal, job-related, or some combination of all three. Regardless, one must possess the requisite skills to produce the results in whatever arena one focuses.

The rub, though, is that there are tons of people who possess all the skills: they've read the books, attended the seminars, been coached by experts. Yet they still do not produce extraordinary results. Why? It finally dawned on me that it is because they are deficient or defective in some critical aspect of their character. This prohibits them from sufficiently developing and / or relentlessly using their skills to their full advantage.

The root Source of greatness, then, comes not from skillfulness, though skills are necessary. It comes not from motivation, because motivation in the form

Results

Means

Source

Greatness
(However One
Defines It)

Skillfulness

Character

FIGURE 1.2 The Tree of Extraordinary Performance and Results

of dedication and determination by itself is not sustainable. It comes from character. With the requisite character traits in place, a person will be relentless in using the skills necessary to produce the intended great results. In the end, there is an intimate connection between who one is at one's core and what one does. So producing treasured results starts with the inner core of a person – that is, his or her character – and then moves to the outer world of dedicated, determined hard work.

CHARACTER AND UNRELENTING DRIVE, DEDICATION, AND DETERMINATION

If you looked up the word "character" in the dictionary, you would find any number of definitions. Some include: one of the attributes that make up and distinguish an individual; one's reputation; moral excellence and firmness.

But the definition that best serves our purpose is supplied by the Merriam-Webster dictionary (2015). It states that character is "the complex of mental traits that make and individualize a person" (p. 126). This definition suggests several useful things and paves the way for developing Unrelenting Drive, Dedication, and Determination.

1. Defining character nonjudgmentally as "a complex of mental traits," it suggests first that everybody possesses character. Jesus of Nazareth, Mahatma Gandhi, and Mother Teresa all did, as did Adolf Hitler, Charles Manson, and Osama bin Laden. The question is not, "Is this a person of character?" It is, "What are the mental states that make up this person's character?"

   By way of example, let's contrast statements made by Benito Mussolini and Mother Teresa, statements we can assume to represent a core mental trait of each. Mussolini once said, "Let us have a dagger between our teeth, a bomb in our hands, and an infinite scorning in our hearts." Taken as a core belief, what could we say about his character? How would we predict he would act across situations?

   Now take a look at a famous statement Mother Teresa made: "Kind words can be short and easy to speak, but their echoes are truly endless." What does this way of thinking tell us about her character? Holding this belief, how would we predict she'd deal with people?

   Both these individuals had strong characters. But, one's led to death and destruction, the other's to compassion and tenderness.

2. This definition of character suggests, second, that the mental traits one possesses largely drive how one conducts oneself in life. By knowing

Activates   Causes

A ═══════════════➤ B ═══════════════➤ C

Activating Event   Beliefs   Consequences
                          (Mental Traits)

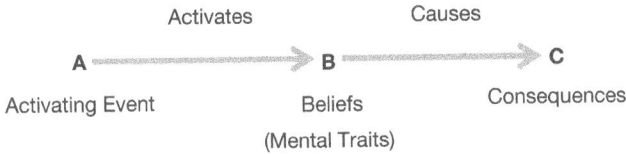

FIGURE 1.3   The ABCs of Character

exactly the mental traits of Mahatma Gandhi and Osama bin Laden –
each of their core, deeply endorsed beliefs, principles, or paradigms – we
could not only define their character, but quite accurately predict their
behavior across a wide variety of situations. Conversely, by observing
their behavior over time, we could make educated guesses about their
foundational mental paradigms, principles, and beliefs.

This can be conceptualized in the ABC model of Rational Emotive
Behavior Therapy (REBT), as illustrated in Figure 1.3. In this figure, A represents the events we encounter in our daily life – some significant but
others inconsequential, some common but others unusual. B represents
the core beliefs we endorse as true and valid through our life experiences.
These beliefs can be cold ("This *is* butter pecan ice cream"), warm
("I *like/dislike* butter pecan ice cream"), or hot ("I *have to* have it/avoid
it."). C then represents the behavioral, emotional, and/or physiological
reactions to the events we encounter in our day-to-day life.

What we have learned from literally thousands upon thousands
of research studies is that it is not the events at A that directly cause us
to react as we do at C. Rather, it is our beliefs at B. You see, everything
we encounter in the world at A has to pass through our beliefs to be
processed – i.e., perceived, comprehended, judged – before we react at C.
To put it another way, we react at C depending on the Bs that get
activated by the A.

Take Smith and Jones, who both walk down the street and spot a fat
wallet lying on the street (an A). Smith thinks, "Wow, look at that wallet
– finders keepers, losers weepers" (his B). Simultaneously, Jones thinks,
"I don't care how much money that wallet holds – it's not mine, and the
right thing is to return it to its owner" (his B). Same wallet (A), but two
different thought patterns (B). Predictably, Smith would be spurred to
keep the wallet (C), while Jones would likely try to find its owner (C).

REBT therapists, like myself, work with this ABC model every day.
We know that most all the emotional and behavioral problems we treat
are not caused by our patients' difficult life circumstances, but by the
irrational beliefs these people have deeply endorsed and thusly apply to
their circumstances. Our therapeutic thrust is to use our technology

to help our patients first identify, then eradicate, and finally replace their dysfunctional beliefs with more rational and efficacious ones.

It would follow, then, that if we wanted to get a clear picture of the quality of a person's character, we'd want to identify a person's most profoundly endorsed beliefs. Knowing this, we'd be able to fairly accurately understand why a person acts as he/she does, makes the choices he/she makes, treats others the way he/she does. Similarly, by observing a person's behavior over time, we'd be able to make some pretty educated guesses about the key characterological beliefs (traits) that person holds.

3. Character, thusly defined as mental traits or core beliefs, can be developed and grown. What we have to do is first articulate the belief that would both define that character trait and then go about the process of teaching that belief until it is endorsed, ingrained, and regularly acted upon – through explaining, modeling, practicing, and reinforcing. This is exactly what *Developing Unrelenting Drive, Dedication, and Determination* does in the succeeding chapters.

Summarized below, then, are the seven character traits that are the root source of developing Unrelenting Drive, Dedication, and Determination. They are learnable and sustainable, regardless of one's age, experience, and station, and they work.

Unconditional Personal Responsibility (Chapter 2)

Unconditional Personal Responsibility (UPR) is a character trait that, once embraced, leads to no-holds-barred, sustained action until desired results are produced. It is the principle whereby you act according to your commitments, not to your transient feelings or the outside circumstances you encounter. Adopting the belief that the center of life is your commitments, not your feelings, your psychological make-up, or even your past experiences, you commit to doing what you say you will do, despite any difficult circumstances you encounter. You then push through obstacles and persist as long as necessary, without making excuses or surrendering to the pressure of others or circumstances, just doing what is necessary until desired results are produced.

Passionate Purpose (Chapter 3)

Once you determine that the important results you want are an expression of your life's purpose, you cannot help but bring drive, dedication, and determination to each day's efforts. You will be driven to act relentlessly to meet cherished goals, all the while feeling rewarded, satisfied, and even joyful in the process.

Fearlessness (Chapter 4)

Fears of failure ravage initiative and effort. Why? Because such fears are almost always ego-bound. For, in your belief system, when you connect your self-worth to succeeding at something, you will have such fear of failure that you are driven to pull back from boldness. By playing it safe, you avoid failure, but you block the possibility for great results. Freeing yourself from ego opens the door to the open-throttle effort needed to give greatness a chance.

Interpersonal Intelligence (Chapter 5)

Interpersonal Intelligence is not about being socially adept or interpersonally skillful. After all, sociopaths can be quite charming. Interpersonal Intelligence is about adopting the kinds of beliefs that lead one to genuinely hold value for other people, habitually relate to them in an affirming, respectful way, and appreciate them for who they are. With the conviction that we live in an interdependent world in which we can best achieve great results with the loyalty, cooperation, and help of others, these types of beliefs serve to generate goodwill, cooperation, and trust in others.

Mental Muscle (Chapter 6)

People with Unrelenting Drive, Dedication, and Determination are mentally tough. They have grit and resilience. They have learned exactly how to stay focused on achieving their goals in the face of adversity. They know how to sustain effort even when frustrated. In short, they have ingrained the kind of beliefs that promote sustained, extraordinary effort no matter what.

Robust Vitality (Chapter 7)

Virtually everyone who produces great results possesses high energy and vitality. Some are genetically blessed in this department, while others have to work to acquire and maintain it. This sixth trait has to do with the attitudes and strategies to keep renewed and refreshed – mentally, emotionally, physically.

Harmony at Home (Chapter 8)

A person's primary relationship can be a strong wind in the sails or a millstone around the neck. Building Harmony at Home requires three mindsets: Premeditated Acceptance and Forgiveness; Relentless and Intelligent Giving; and 100% Relationship Responsibility.

Armed with these seven character traits, one is primed to sustain the Unrelenting Drive, Dedication, and Determination needed to produce the fruits of greatness, however one personally defines them. In each of the next seven chapters, I will explain a trait, show you how to grow it, help you develop your own personal action plan to put it to immediate use, and, as a bonus, illustrate how I have successfully applied it in an organizational setting.

HOW TO USE THIS BOOK

Whether you are a helping professional or a layperson, I want you to know how honored I am to share with you the concepts and tools in this book. Even though I do not personally know you, I assure you that I have put my heart and soul into it.

Think of this book as a combined seminar and workshop. It is a seminar in that I will provide you with concepts, principles, and tools that you can put to immediate use to help others or yourself develop the Unrelenting Drive, Dedication, and Determination you need to produce extraordinary results. It is also a workshop in that I will guide you through opportunities to self-reflect, self-assess, plan, and make action commitments to implement the presented ideas and tools in daily life.

In writing this book, I have done my very best to communicate the content of each character trait in an accessible, enjoyable, and intelligent manner. I have tried to keep you involved on every page and to spur your enrollment. However, I can only do so much. Picture yourself attending a banquet: I'll supply the food, but you need to bring the utensils. They are three in number:

1. **Be responsible.** Each of the chapters in this book stands alone. You can tackle them in order, or you can hop around focusing on the ones that seem most applicable to you. Regardless of how you proceed, you must do your part in three ways: (1) actively and energetically think about how to apply what I will teach you to your life; (2) follow through on all the exercises in the workshop section of each chapter; (3) follow through regularly on the action plans you develop. After all, producing the greatness in the life you want is your job.

2. **Be open.** There is perhaps nothing more crippling to growth than closed-mindedness. We all have a tendency to be committed to what we already know, believing that our pre-existing way of thinking and doing is not only the right way but the only way. While we each know a lot, an attitude of knowing can be self-limiting, for when we take the perspective that we already know, we are not open to new ideas. It is powerful to take the stance, "I don't know, and I know I don't know." By "not knowing," you will be open to new, valuable information.

3. **Be fun loving.** What will be presented to you in this book, I think, is both interesting and useful. It truly can make a profound difference in your life. Nonetheless, don't take it or yourself too seriously. Have fun. Enjoy the ride. The more you can balance lightheartedness with seriousness, the more you will get out of what is offered.

GOING FORWARD

Before launching, I want you to know that you absolutely can produce the great results you want in your life. Maybe you will never replicate the public greatness of a Michael Jordan, an Igor Stravinsky, or a Bill Gates. But, you can achieve greatness, however you define it, within your own personal sphere of influence, once you put in place these requisite character traits.

Now it is up to you. You can without question internalize and more importantly use each of these character traits to produce your greatness. I know you can do it. Will you? It's up to you. Go for it!

REFERENCES AND SUGGESTED READING

Collins, J. (2001). *Good to great*. New York: HarperCollins.

Colvin, G. (2008). *Talent is overrated: What really separates world-class performers from everybody else*. New York: Penguin.

Covey, S. R. (2006). *Everyday greatness*. Nashville, TN: Rutledge Hill Press.

Gladwell, M. (2008). *Outliers: The story of success*. New York: Little, Brown & Company.

Kroc, R. (1977). *Grinding it out: The making of McDonald's*. New York: St. Martin's Press.

Marden, O. S. (1907). *The optimistic life*. New York: Thomas Y. Crowell & Co. Publishers.

Weizmann, C. (2013). *Trial and error: The autobiography of Chaim Weizmann*. New York: Plunkett Lake Press.

CHAPTER 2

Unconditional Personal Responsibility

The royal road to great results – living by
your word, outside of circumstances

People are always blaming their circumstances for what they are. I don't believe in circumstances.
The people who get on in the world are the people who get up and look for the circumstances
they want and if they can't find them, make them.

George Bernard Shaw

Unconditional Personal Responsibility (UPR) is the granddaddy of developing Unrelenting Drive, Dedication, and Determination. By mastering this character trait, a person will be absolutely dedicated to sustaining the necessary effort to produce desired results. He or she will persist despite the ups and downs of moods, unexpected adversities, or any personal shortcomings.

Does this sound pie-in-the-sky? It's not, for many, many people have succeeded as a result of possessing this character trait. Take Andrew Wiles, a mathematics professor at Princeton University. Story has it that the ten-year-old Wiles became fascinated with the French mathematician Pierre de Fermat's Last Theorem. Being a prodigy, he spent his childhood studying how mathematical scholars of earlier ages approached this theorem, putting aside most all of the typical interests of his peers.

For those of you non-mathematicians, Fermat had observed some 375 years earlier that, though there are solutions to the equation $x^2 + y^2 = z^2$, there are no solutions if the numbers are cubed rather than squared. In fact, he asserted that he had proof that the equation $x^n + y^n = z^n$ had no solution if "n" is any number larger than 2. The rub, however, was that Fermat never put the evidence to support his theorem on paper. This stimulated three centuries of scholars to try to discover the proof.

Back to Andrew Wiles. After completing his mathematics training, he knuckled down to his academic career. But in 1986, when a colleague showed how solving a particular math hypothesis might contribute to proving Fermat's Last Theorem, Professor Wiles jumped back into the quest. Except for teaching his classes, he devoted the next seven years – more than 15,000 intense hours – to proving Fermat right. Finally, in 1993, he solved it and presented the completed proof to an esteemed conference of colleagues.

Obviously, Professor Wiles was gifted with superior intellect. It is said that only one in 1,000 mathematicians were able to understand his work. But, there had to be more. When somebody asked him how he did it, he summed it up in one word: "Persistence." Keeping Wiles in mind, let's now flesh out what exactly the character trait of Unconditional Personal Responsibility is.

DEFINING UNCONDITIONAL PERSONAL RESPONSIBILITY

It is important to emphasize that Unconditional Personal Responsibility does not refer to something tangible, such as a chore, like cleaning your room, or a duty, like paying your bills in a timely fashion. Rather, it is a profound character trait – a foundational belief, paradigm, or principle – that one either adopts and lives by or doesn't.

A First Definition of Unconditional Personal Responsibility

The following definition of Unconditional Personal Responsibility was originally created by the EST Foundation. Read it carefully, then I'll do my best to help you make sense of it.

> Responsibility starts with the **willingness** to experience your **self** as **cause**. It starts with the **willingness** to have the experience of your **self** as **cause** in the matter.
> Responsibility is not burden, fault, praise, blame, credit, shame, or guilt. All these include judgments and evaluations of right or wrong, better or worse, or being a good or bad person. They are not responsibility. [. . .]
> Responsibility starts with the **willingness** to deal with a situation from and with the point of view, whether at the moment realized or not, that **you** are the **cause**, or source, of what you are, what you do, and what you have. [. . .]
> Ultimately, responsibility is a principle – a principle of **self** as source – for what you choose to do. (Erhard, 1979)

You will notice that this definition contains three significant concepts, all in bold: willingness, self, and cause. Let's now flesh these out.

Willingness

Unconditional Personal Responsibility starts with a person being *willing to do whatever is necessary* – whatever that may be, within, of course, the confines of ethics, morals, safety, and the law – to produce intended results. Distinct from trying, which focuses on effort but not results, doing what is necessary emphasizes sustaining action until the intended results are produced. Thus, one who lives by the character trait of UPR persists, persists, persists until the results are created. That is exactly what Andrew Wiles did. He was willing to do what was necessary.

Let me concretize this with an example. A few years ago, I suffered from pain in my hip that was so excruciating that it greatly curtailed my mobility. When rest and ice failed to fix the problem, I consulted an orthopedic surgeon. This specialist listened to my story, poked and probed, and, after offhandedly mentioning that he could not x-ray my hip because his technician was off for the day, told me I suffered from trocantric bursitis. He gave me a shot of cortisone, told me I would soon be fine, and sent me on my way.

Finding no relief after a couple of weeks, I met him a second time with a certain degree of urgency as I was about to depart on a week-long consulting trip to the Caribbean, a trip I most certainly didn't want to face with such pain. I got even less satisfaction this second time around, except for his reiteration that my problem was indeed bursitis and the assurance that rest, warm air, and salt water would do the trick. Slam, bam, thank you ma'am.

I'm sure you've figured out that I returned from my trip a week later with my hip still throbbing. With a great deal of frustration (and, I might add, exhaustion from being unable to sleep), I visited my regular physician who promised me that he wouldn't rest until he got my hip healed. He proceeded to guide me through a series of tests until he identified the exact cause of my pain (which, thank goodness, was merely muscular). He then directed me to a physical therapist who worked with me until the mission was accomplished. I might add that my family doctor had his nurse call me on a weekly basis to monitor my progress.

Please be clear that this story is not about medical competence. It is about personal responsibility. The orthopedist's mindset had to do with applying his trade. His commitment was to his medical procedures, not to doing what was necessary to produce the desired result. Trying was the coin of the realm for him, with results being incidental to his actions. The family physician, cut from the mold of Andrew Wiles, knew that results were all that mattered. He committed to persist in doing what was necessary to produce the results he and I both wanted. He used the tools of his trade in the service of producing these results, not as an end in and of themselves. Thank goodness this second professional passed the willingness muster of the character trait of Unconditional Personal Responsibility.

Self

You may recall that the first sentence of the EST Foundation's definition of Unconditional Personal Responsibility is, "Responsibility starts with the willingness to experience your self as cause." Guess to whom "self" refers? That's right, you. In the world of Unconditional Personal Responsibility, you, and no one else, are the source, or cause, of whatever you do or don't do – not other people, not what happens around you, not even what goes on inside you (i.e., your current feelings or motivational state). Think of it: in any situation, you are always the chooser of the choice you choose. In the realm of Unconditional Personal Responsibility, this is unconditional and absolute.

Imagine, for example, that you and I meet for dinner. After we part, an armed robber pops out of the shadows and demands that I give him my valuables. Not being stupid, I of course do so, a decision I'm sure you would agree is intelligent. I give up my billfold and watch, but I hold onto my life.

But, let's say that, after an understandably restless night, I ring you the next morning and tell you, "You won't believe what happened last night. On the way to my car, some guy put a gun to my head and said, 'Your money or your life.' What can I say, he forced me to give him every penny I had on me."

Note the lack of personal responsibility in what I said. The fact is that the robber in no way made me give him my valuables. What he did was present me with a choice: I could choose to give him my possessions, or I could choose to refuse. Of course, this latter choice would have been ill-advised, even if I were James Bond. By all reasonable logic, I made the better of the two choices. But, the point is that I was the chooser of the choice I chose. To say it another way, I was 100% responsible for my choice, which was to intelligently give him my valuables.

You see, we always have choice. This is so whether contending with relatively inconsequential matters, such as deciding to sleep in rather than pushing out of bed to exercise, or with major issues, such as with my made-up robbery vignette. This basic truth – that I am responsible for every one of my choices – is one of the most empowering realizations a person can make. For, when one accepts this, one claims the power to do what is necessary to produce the results one wants. Ask Professor Wiles if this isn't true. He chose how he spent his time until he solved Fermat's Last Theorem.

So, let's sum up what we've learned about Unconditional Personal Responsibility so far. First, UPR starts with a person being staunchly willing to do whatever it takes to produce an intended result. This stance drives him or her to keep doing until the result is produced. Second, the person takes full responsibility for all of his or her choices. This person knows that he or she always has a choice and, furthermore, it is himself or herself that always makes every choice he or she makes.

These two UPR ingredients – willingness and self – then set the stage for the last component of Unconditional Personal Responsibility: cause. It is one of the most important concepts one will ever learn in one's life.

Cause

UPR makes a critical distinction between the concept of *cause*, more completely stated as *Being at Cause*, the embodiment of Unconditional Personal Responsibility, and effect, or *Being at Effect*, the essence of Conditional Personal Responsibility. To really understand Being at Cause, let's first flesh out its mirror opposite, Being at Effect. Being at Effect can be captured by the following statement:

> How I act, the choices I make, and the results I produce ultimately depend on the circumstances operating at the time. So, when I give my word to do something, or commit to producing some result, I do mean it. I'm not lying. But, I know, in the back of my mind, that, if some circumstance arises that makes it difficult or unpleasant to keep my promise, that circumstance justifies not keeping it.

To illustrate, go back to our dinner date. Let's say that, during our conversation, you requested and I committed to help you move a few pieces of heavy furniture to a storage unit the next morning at 10.00 a.m. We then part, I get robbed, and I go home stressed out and unable to sleep.

Forward to the next morning. At 8.00 a.m., dead tired and bleary eyed, I call you to beg off. I explain what happened, apologize profusely, and offer to help once I get some rest. You, as expected, respond graciously. You express understanding, tell me not to worry about it, and offer to be supportive in any way you can.

Sounds good, doesn't it? But, consider that there are different levels to this story. On a social level, both you and I behaved exemplarily: I called you as soon as I got out of bed, did my best to let you know I hadn't intended to inconvenience you, and humbly apologized. You, in turn, were empathic and supportive. Interpersonally, we both did well.

But, look at what took place at the level of Unconditional Personal Responsibility. From beginning to end, I acted irresponsibly. What I communicated, first to myself and then to you, was that my commitment to you was conditional; that is, under the adverse circumstances of being tired, my commitment to help you became null and void. With this "Being at Effect" mindset, my obligation to you was fulfilled when I gave you my reasons for begging off – explaining to you my dilemma and expressing regret. Game, set, match.

Guess what, though? I broke my word, I did not choose to act to honor my promise. And you did not get your furniture moved. No result.

For those of you who think my comments inhumane, I hasten to emphasize that I could have easily chosen to fulfill my commitment. Though tired, I could have dragged myself to your house, lugged furniture for an hour or two, and then gone home for a good, long nap. Big deal. I once ran the New York Marathon on very little sleep. I could have fulfilled my promise to produce the result had I held my commitment at a higher value than my personal comfort.

| Being at Effect | vs. | Being at Cause |
(Conditional Personal Responsibility)		(Unconditional Personal Responsibility)

• Live by circumstances
• Live by your psychology –
  feelings, desires, and habits
• Results by luck, hope, or prayer
• Excuses instead of results
  are acceptable
		• Live by your word/commitment
		• Live by your character –
		  principles
		• Results on purpose
		• No excuses valid or acceptable;
		  only results

FIGURE 2.1   The Conditional/Unconditional Personal Responsibility Dichotomy

And to not let you off the hook, you did no better with regard to UPR than I did. You also affirmed that the unspoken rule of our relationship was that the commitments we make to each other are breakable, depending on the circumstances. Furthermore, you probably didn't want to hold me accountable for my promises because that would give me permission to expect you to unconditionally honor yours in the future as well.

So, Being at Effect is a mindset – a belief, paradigm, or principle – in which one views one's promises or commitments as always bendable or breakable, depending on the circumstance that exists at the moment of truth. If the circumstances are benign or favorable, of course the person will act; if not, then one produces excuses ("I'm just too tired"), blame ("The robber made it impossible"), or whining ("Things just never work out my way"), but not results. The lost results were miniscule in this one example, but imagine the massive amount of missed results over a lifetime with this way of thinking.

As I'm sure you've gathered by now, the concept of Being at Cause is key to Unconditional Personal Responsibility. It is about making choices outside circumstances. It means that your word – your promise, your commitment – is the driving force of your choices, not your inner state or the outer world of people, places, or things. It is being willing to do whatever it takes to produce promised results, no matter what the circumstances. It is a life of integrity and intended results.

A Second Definition of Unconditional Personal Responsibility

For those of you adverse to psychobabble, here's another definition of Unconditional Personal Responsibility in more down-to-earth language:

Responsibility is a **belief** in which one holds oneself **100% responsible** for honoring one's promises and commitments and producing intended results, no matter how hard it may be.

Responsibility is being **100% willing** to rise above difficult circumstances to achieve the results one promises. It is a belief in which one continually asks, "What else can I do to overcome these obstacles and problems and keep my promised and committed results?"

Ultimately, responsibility is a **belief** one holds that says, "My word is my bond, and I will keep my word even when it is tough to do so."

Both the first and the second definitions illuminate the five key aspects of Unconditional Personal Responsibility:

1. *You are driven by your word*, not by the inner circumstances of your psychology – your comfort, your desires for approval, your motivational level – or the circumstances outside you – the traffic, the telephone, other people's actions. Think about UPR being contextualized within three concentric circles, as illustrated in Figure 2.2. The innermost circle represents a specific commitment you make, as in, "I will be at your house tomorrow at 10.00 a.m. to help you move your furniture." Consistent with everything already said, you would unconditionally fulfill this commitment if you honored UPR.

    The middle circle represents all the character principles you hold near and dear, such as honesty, generosity, or courage. The point here is never to make a specific commitment that is contrary to your principles because this puts you in a no-win situation – for if you honor your specific commitment, you violate one of your principles, but if you honor your principles, you do not keep your commitment.

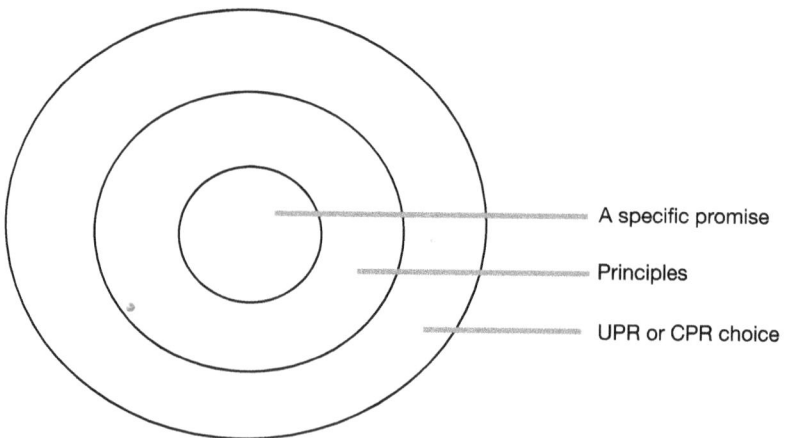

FIGURE 2.2   UPR: Commitment to Commitment

The outermost circle represents the character-based choice between Conditional or Unconditional Personal Responsibility. It contextualizes everything. Assuming you make the UPR choice, this choice becomes your Super Principle. Why do I call it a Super Principle? Because, if you commit to live by the principle of UPR, you will almost always honor all your other principles, as well as all your specific promises. In essence, Unconditional Personal Responsibility boils down to a commitment to honor your commitments as the guiding light of your life.

2. Neither the size of your commitment, the degree of its importance, nor to whom it is made (including to yourself) makes any difference. *The only thing that matters is that you made a commitment.* Once made, no circumstance, outside or inside you, justifies not keeping it.

3. Once a promise is given or a commitment is made, *your focus is on no-holds-barred doing.* Your attitude should be: (1) I will *do* what I need to do to keep my promise; (2) I will willingly *persist* until I fulfill all the conditions of my promise. I might add here that, as with Andrew Wiles, the concept of persistence repeats itself over and over again in success stories. Albert Einstein famously said, "Genius is 10% inspiration and 90% perspiration." Babe Ruth once remarked, "It's hard to beat somebody who never gives up."

4. *Obstacles are never game-breakers.* They are merely things to overcome to produce the promised results. The questions a person who owns UPR repeatedly ask are: What else can I do? How can I overcome this obstacle and produce my commitment results? Who or what do I need to enlist if I can't do it on my own?

5. Carefully choose what promises you make. But, once you make them, hold them sacred and fulfill them.

THE UNCONDITIONAL PERSONAL RESPONSIBILITY WORKSHOP

Now is the opportunity to put Unconditional Personal Responsibility into practice. If you are a clinician, consultant, or coach, you can work your client through this workshop in two ways: you can do it together in your office, or you can assign it to be done before your next appointment and then review it together. If you are a client or someone doing this on your own, be sure you do it with integrity and energy, for this six-step workshop gives you an opportunity to produce the great results you want.

With apologies for sounding hyperbolic, the decisions made by you or your client in this workshop will have a profound impact vis-à-vis you or your client's potential for leaving a legacy of great results. Therefore, I want to introduce this UPR workshop by asserting two things:

1. You have two and only two choices in the domain of personal responsibility: you either fully commit to and completely live by Unconditional Personal Responsibility, thereby delivering the promised results despite the hardships that exist; or you live by Conditional Personal Responsibility, doing what is necessary to produce results, but only when it is easy or convenient. You cannot be kind of committed to your commitments any more than you can be kind of pregnant. It's all or none, black or white, one way or the other.

2. You cannot avoid the choice between UPR and CPR. Every day of your life, whether you realize it or not, you have chosen and lived by one or the other of these two paradigms. The truth is that you cannot avoid making this life-determining decision. So, you might as well step up to the plate and make it consciously and on purpose.

Step One: Assure Understanding

Step One is straightforward and simple. You are to answer these two questions: (1) Do I understand the distinction between Unconditional Personal Responsibility (Being at Cause) and Conditional Personal Responsibility (Being at Effect)? (2) If not, exactly what is my confusion or what questions do I need to ask to get clarification? Write down below anything you need to know to fully understand the distinction between these two responsibility paradigms. Please note that you are welcome to contact me should you have any questions or concerns.

_____

_____

_____

_____

_____

Step Two: Develop Self-Awareness

Step Two is a more personal exercise and has two parts. To start, first identify three recent situations in which you made a promise or commitment and did not keep it. These could be promises you made to others or even to yourself; they may be well thought out or ones made on the spur of the moment; they may be large or small. For each, write the reasons you gave to yourself and/or to another person to excuse, explain, or rationalize why you did not keep it. Above all, be forthcoming, as we all break promises.

Broken Promise   **Reason**

1. _____   _____
   _____   _____
   _____   _____
   _____   _____

2. _____   _____
   _____   _____
   _____   _____
   _____   _____

3. _____   _____
   _____   _____
   _____   _____
   _____   _____

Good. Now, for each of these three broken promises or commitments, figure out exactly how you could have kept them, despite the difficulties you faced. When I conduct this step with a live audience, I find that most participants discover that they can bat 100% if they really decide to put comfort and convenience aside. I bet you can too. I challenge you to do this. Go for it!

1. _____
   _____
   _____

2. _____
   _____
   _____

3. _____
   _____
   _____

If I'm correct, you, like my seminar people, found that you indeed could have kept each of your three broken promises, though to do so might have caused you some hardship. Assuming I'm correct, I've backed you into a corner. You made the commitment and did not keep it, but you proved you could. The questions I now ask you are: Why didn't you keep your word? What kept you from honoring your promise?

When I ask these questions to my live attendees, I almost always get a slew of reasons that break down into three categories: (1) "To keep my commitment would have caused me hardship"; (2) "My priorities changed such that other things became more important"; (3) "I simply didn't feel like it." Do these sound familiar? Which ones did you use in your examples?

These reasons all follow the PITA principle: it was a Pain In The A_ _. In other words, psychologically speaking, you found it too frustrating and/or you were no longer sufficiently motivated to follow through. But, even deeper, the character-based reason was that you were in the grip of the paradigm of Conditional Personal Responsibility (Being at Effect). With this paradigm, you succumbed to the circumstances; you chose to not act to produce the result you promised, thereby outside integrity. If you had held the paradigm of Unconditional Personal Responsibility, you would have acted to keep your word by producing the promised result despite the difficulties involved.

I hope Step Two has raised your consciousness as to where you stand on personal responsibility and to the seductive power of Being at Effect. I also hope it has piqued your interest to move forward to Step Three.

Step Three: Become Able

We all face difficult circumstances that tempt us to break our word. Our ability to overcome these circumstances depends on being aware of them and on having a plan to ignore or overcome them. Below is an opportunity for you to inventory your circumstantial life. What are those inner and outer circumstances in your life that you let block you from doing what is necessary to produce your results? For each, what will you do to ignore or eliminate them going forward?

Inner Circumstances	Action Plan

- Negative feeling states:

  _____   _____
  _____   _____

- Diminished motivation:

  _____   _____
  _____   _____

- Body conditions:

  _____   _____
  _____   _____

- Changing priorities:

  _____   _____
  _____   _____

Outer Circumstances	**Action Plan**
• People:	
_____	_____
_____	_____
• Places:	
_____	_____
_____	_____
• Things:	
_____	_____
_____	_____

Step Four: Determine Willingness

Step Four is where the rubber hits the road. It is the heart of the UPR workshop. This is where you are asked to make the decision as to which paradigm, Unconditional or Conditional Personal Responsibility, you will commit to live by – consciously, no-holds-barred. Please understand that you have only two choices, UPR or CPR, each represented by one of these two pledges that follow. Unfortunately, you cannot choose to not make this choice. There are no shades of gray. If you are not willing to unconditionally honor your word, then you are, by default, choosing to only keep your word conditionally. That is, alas, the human condition.

Read the two pledges below. Sign and date one or the other. Remember, if you are not willing to pledge to the first, then you have automatically defaulted to the second, so you might as well make it explicit by signing it.

I, _____, take full responsibility for and fully commit to keeping all my promises and commitments, both to others and to myself. I will hereafter live fully committed to my commitments, despite adverse circumstances.

Signed _____

Date _____

I, _____, take full responsibility for and fully commit to keeping all my promises and commitments, both to others and to myself, so long as it is convenient to do so. I will hereafter live fully committed to my commitments, but only if the circumstances make it easy for me to do so, if nothing better comes along, and/or I still feel like it.

Signed _____

Date _____

Step Five: Do on Purpose

Hopefully you mustered the courage and commitment to sign the first pledge. Step Five gets concrete. How will you implement Unconditional Personal Responsibility in your life? Specifically write one to three commitments you will make both in your personal life and in your professional life, ones that you will hereafter honor despite difficult circumstances. Two suggestions: (1) make meaningful commitments, ones that make a difference and/or ones that you have to date been weak in keeping; (2) be careful to not overwhelm yourself with too many commitments or overly taxing ones that set you up for failure (i.e., you may need to give yourself time to build your UPR muscle).

	Personal	**Professional**
1.	_____	_____
2.	_____	_____
3.	_____	_____

Step Six: Gather Your Support

Living by your word is very difficult, particularly when you first get started. It will help to have the support of people who are committed to helping you keep your commitments along the way. Years ago, a group of friends and I organized a support group we called CACA – the Charlottesville Association for Committed Action. The sole purpose of CACA was to help each other honor our commitments. I'm happy to report that we all found ourselves most productive during the life of this group.

This last step in your UPR workshop has two parts to it. First, identify a person or persons you will ask to support you in conducting your life consistent with Unconditional Personal Responsibility. Select them with care because these people are to apply tough love to you, not warm huggies that enable you to make excuses when you choose not to act with integrity.

Then, note exactly what you will request they do to support you in this endeavor.

Support Person(s)	My Request
1. _____	_____
	_____
	_____
2. _____	_____
	_____
	_____
3. _____	_____
	_____
	_____

Congratulations for completing this workshop. It has provided you with a springboard to developing your Unconditional Personal Responsibility muscle and thereby doing what is necessary to achieve the great results you want in your life.

INTENSIFIERS

What follows are three Intensifiers to deepen your ability to live by your word. Think how you can integrate each of these into your daily routine.

Build Your UPR Muscle

With no disrespect intended, I doubt that you have heard personal responsibility explained the way I have in this chapter. So, it is likely that you have some muscle building to do to ingrain UPR into your decision-making patterns.

You can approach this muscle building in one of two ways. One might be called transformational. This means that you go whole hog; you determine right now to keep every one of your commitments – 100% – from this moment forward. You step totally into the UPR paradigm and don't look back.

The second approach is developmental. This means that you start first by making and keeping small commitments; then, as you gain strength and confidence, you gradually increase the number and weight of your commitment-keeping until you become really strong at it.

Whatever approach you take, be alert for those moments of truth when you are tempted to break a commitment. At these moments, watch for your excuse-making self-talk, refute these CPR messages, and then act to honor your promise at all costs. These moments of truth provide wonderful opportunities to build muscle.

Put Teeth in Your Promises

We often make promises that are very weak; they sound more like hopes, wishes, and maybes rather than true-blue promises. How often do we say things like "We'll see," "I'll do my best," or "I'll try"?

Promises with teeth in them, ones that come from the principle of Unconditional Personal Responsibility, follow this formula: "I promise (you) that I will do X by time Y." Notice that this way of making promises contains these elements:

- "I" – you put yourself at risk by owning the promise. You are willing to take a stand and be committed to producing the promised results.
- "Promise" – by using the word "promise," you take a stand. You have put your integrity on the line. You have stated, in no uncertain terms, a no-holds-barred commitment. Similar words to "promise" would be "pledge," "swear," "assure," "guarantee," "commit," and the like.
- "I will" – "I will" serves to underscore your willingness to do what is necessary to produce the promised results.
- Conditions of satisfaction – these are the promised results, telling exactly what you promise to do and by precisely what time you will deliver. This leaves no wiggle room and tells the receiver of the promise exactly what to expect.

So, when making a promise, be sure to make it powerful. Following the above formula serves you well on two fronts: (1) it keeps you alert to the fact that you are indeed making a promise; and (2) it leaves no question in your mind, as well as in the mind of the recipient of your promise, what you are committed to doing.

Do a Weekly Check-In

You would be wise to keep tabs on yourself by evaluating how faithfully you act with Unconditional Personal Responsibility. I find Sunday evening the best time for me to do my check-in. On Sunday, I review the previous week with regard to how well I did in keeping my word, and I recommit to those promises I may have let slip. I also use this time to reflect on the upcoming week, noting commitments I have made that are due that week. Scheduling a weekly check-in for yourself can also serve you well. It will help you build your UPR muscle and keep you focused on maintaining your integrity.

AN ORGANIZATIONAL CASE STUDY

Martin Horn, Inc. is a family-owned construction company located in Charlottesville, Virginia. It has built homes and buildings of great beauty and function for decades throughout the area. Perhaps its crowning achievement is the Pavilion, an outdoor amphitheater that sits on the far east end of Charlottesville's downtown pedestrian mall. Sloping from back to front toward the stage and covered by a billowy white tarp that gives it the look of a giant covered wagon, it has welcomed such name acts as Willie Nelson, Crosby, Stills & Nash, Harry Connick Jr., Bonnie Raitt, Prairie Home Companion, and Dwight Yoakum. It has even hosted the Dalai Lama and President Barack Obama.

My work with Martin Horn started with a day-long workshop with its leadership team – President Jack Horn, Vice-Presidents Doug and Ted Horn, their five project managers, and the Directors of Human Resource and Finance. My task was to help them eradicate the problems of lagging productivity.

The day started focused and intense. I first broke the ten of them into two groups of five. I assigned them the task of identifying and describing "the major problems that had that kept them from being the best they can be."

After a half hour or so, we reassembled and I wrote on the whiteboard the seven problems they collectively identified. Then the fun began.

"Okay," I said, "let's take this first one. How long has this problem existed?"

There was a pause before someone piped up, "Forever." Several people chuckled.

"Do you all agree?" I said.

"Yeahs" came from all around.

I wrote the word "Forever" next to the first problem and led the group down the remaining six. To the same question as before, the answer was identical: "Forever."

I knew I had arrived at a moment of truth for them. I felt a knot grow in my stomach, knowing I had to confront the issue head on, but not knowing how they'd take my feedback. For drama's sake, I looked slowly around the room and in a somber voice asked, "What's wrong with this picture?"

A silence, loud as a train rumble, hung in the room. Everybody stared at me.

After a pause, I said, "Here's what's wrong with this picture. These problems have held you back from being as productive as you could be. You've been aware of them forever. You're the leadership team. And you've not acted to fix them."

The silence felt oppressive. The thought passed through my mind that at any minute I could be jumped and pummeled by an angry mob.

I gathered myself and went on. "Okay, how about we spend the rest of the day figuring out how to eliminate each of these problems so you can get on to being the best damn construction company you can be?"

And that's what we did the rest of the day. I taught them a problem-solving model outlined by Faust, Lyles, and Phillips in their wonderful book *Responsible Managers Get Results* (1998), broke them into subgroups, and assigned each group the task of figuring out a plan to eradicate their problems (one group tackled three problems while the other took on four).

Each group did a fabulous job. Mid-afternoon, they shared their solutions to the whole group, and then added touches here and there to finalize their action plans. Interestingly enough, the solutions they created weren't novel or beyond their knowledge or skill base.

Throughout the day, I knew that helping them solve these specific problems and teaching them the skill of problem-solving were not Martin Horn's core problems. It was an issue of personal responsibility.

After the workshop, I sat down with Jack Horn. He wore khaki pants, a flannel shirt, and loafers, and he sported a long ponytail that hung halfway down his back. A twinkle in his eye gave the final touch to a down-to-earth man with whom I knew I would form a partnership.

I first drew for him the Tree of Extraordinary Performance and Results (p. 7), then explained the critical importance of Unconditional Personal Responsibility at the tree's roots. Finally, I recommended that he think about committing a major effort to integrate UPR into the culture of his company. I suggested that he take some time to think about it, but he surprised me when he said without hesitation, "I don't need to think about it. Let's do it."

I spent the next two years working with Martin Horn on creating a culture of Unconditional Personal Responsibility. Here are the steps they and I took together. If Martin Horn can do it, so can any company willing to do what is necessary.

1. Building an organizational culture of Unconditional Personal Responsibility has to start at the top. Those in top leadership roles must first make two overarching decisions: (1) to make the principle of UPR the guiding light of all policies, procedures, and practices; (2) to be willing to be exemplary models of UPR. Jack had already signed on, but his brothers Doug and Ted made this commitment as well when we met.

2. UPR training was then provided to everyone in the organization, starting with the leadership team (executives, managers, and foremen) and extending all the way down to the front-line employees. The distinction between Being at Cause and Being at Effect was clearly articulated, and the message given, starting that day, that everyone would be held accountable for producing committed results. To give me credibility, Jack introduced me before each workshop session, gave his full endorsement to UPR, and told his workforce that this new paradigm would guide everything done from this point going forward.

3. A ruthless investigation was conducted as to where UPR broke down – that is, where excuses rather than results were either tolerated or, worse, reinforced. These breakdowns had to be fixed. We started first at the organizational level with regard to policies, procedures, and practices, such as hiring, firing, annual review, promotion, and corrective action. Next came the leadership level, coaching anybody who demonstrated weakness in holding those who reported to them responsible for producing committed results. Finally came the personal level with regard to the behavior of each and every individual in the organization.

   This process proved to be laborious. But all those in leadership roles at Martin Horn, in the spirit of UPR, sat down together until all pockets of CPR were identified and a plan of transformation was completed.

4. A no-excuse policy was implemented. Producing committed results had to be the centerpiece of the culture, while excuses could not be tolerated and had to be banished. To accomplish this, Martin Horn's leadership people (project managers, supervisors, and foremen) were trained to be UPR coaches such that, when an employee failed to keep a commitment or produce a promised result, coaching was conducted to grow that person's sense of personal responsibility. The decision was made that those who did not respond to this coaching would be let go.

5. The concept of producing results, on time and of quality, was constantly reinforced. Whenever a task was assigned, the person was asked two questions: (1) Do you understand the assignment? (2) Will you commit to doing it? This set up accountability.

6. Everyone from top to bottom had to be schooled in the necessary skills to meet their responsibilities. For Martin Horn, this started with training for "Holding Conversations for Committed Action," central to which was the proper way to make promises with unconditional commitment for results. Also taught were problem-solving skills at every level of the company. The rule became that circumstances are never an excuse for not producing results and that any problem encountered must be decisively and permanently eliminated. Other skills – e.g., stress management, teamwork, conducting productive meetings – were provided as needed.

It was a pleasure to be associated with such high-character people. Jack Horn and all the people of Martin Horn stepped up to the plate. They embraced the character principle of Unconditional Personal Responsibility to their core. Their results proved it, as they quickly reached the level they wanted and deserved. I felt proud to be a small part of their success.

A FINAL WORD

Unconditional Personal Responsibility is a character trait. It is a core belief or paradigm that says, "I never have to make a promise or a commitment, but, once I do, I will hold that promise or commitment sacred; since I gave my word and put my integrity on the line, I will do whatever it takes to honor it, no matter how difficult it may be." In essence, it shifts the focus from living by such psychological factors as motivation, praise, feelings, or any other circumstance, to living by your word.

People who achieve great results, consciously or unconsciously live by the paradigm of UPR. They, therefore, never give up, persist in the face of adverse circumstances, and bounce back from failure. Conversely, they do not make excuses, whine, self-pity, or blame others or fate for their difficulties. They just do what is necessary because they gave their word to do so.

By building your UPR muscle, you can produce almost any great results you want. All you have to do is be willing to do what is necessary. The great results you want are there to be produced. Unconditional Personal Responsibility is your ticket.

REFERENCES AND SUGGESTED READING

Bate, P. (1994). *Strategies for cultural change*. Oxford: Butterworth-Heinemann.

Connors, R., Smith, T., & Hickman, C. (1994). *The Oz principle*. Englewood Cliffs, NJ: Prentice Hall.

Covey, S. R. (1989). *The 7 habits of highly effective people*. New York: Simon & Schuster.

Erhard, W. (1979). Available at: www.thedragonscave.org/archives/tdc/est/text_files/erhard_quotes2.txt (accessed November 16, 2016).

Eyre, L., & Eyre, R. (1984). *Teaching your children responsibility*. New York: Simon & Schuster.

Faust, G. W., Lyles, R. I., & Phillips, W. (1998). *Responsible managers get results*. New York: American Management Association.

Krzyzewski, M. (2006). *Beyond basketball: Coach K's keywords for success*. New York: Hachette.

Meyer, U. (2015). *Above the line: Lessons in leadership from a championship season*. New York: Penguin.

Sykes, C. J. (1992). *A nation of victims*. New York: St. Martin's Press.

CHAPTER 3

Passionate Purpose

Passion fuels Unrelenting Drive, Dedication, and Determination – but what is it that fuels passion?

But, what do we mean by the American Revolution? Do we mean the American War?
The revolution was affected in the minds and hearts of people.
President John Adams

I want to begin this chapter by sharing a personal story. I have had a relationship with the University of Virginia ever since I came to Charlottesville, Virginia in 1970. For the first ten years, I was a tenured associate professor. Then, when I resigned to go into private practice, I continued this relationship as an adjunct professor through UVa's School of Continuing and Professional Studies.

As an adjunct professor, I regularly taught one- and three-credit courses for businesspeople and professional educators throughout Virginia, but mostly in the northern Virginia area close to Washington DC. I created courses I believed to be engaging, solid in content, and professionally useful. Beyond that, I created courses that I believed had the potential to make a profound difference in the lives of those who enrolled in them.

The long and the short of it was that these courses took on profound meaning to me, much beyond simply being a professional activity. I had a passionate purpose for presenting these courses and totally threw myself into them. As a consequence, I received excellent feedback, had a high percentage of repeat attendees, and got many referrals of new students, not to mention experiencing tons of personal satisfaction.

Then, out of the blue, an unfortunate thing happened. I discovered Georgetown. For those of you who may not be familiar with Georgetown, it's a quaint suburb of DC, replete with both upscale restaurants and drinking saloons, art galleries, cozy coffeehouses, and retail stores of all shapes and sizes. Without being aware of it, little by little my reason for teaching the classes shifted from contributing to people's lives to being an excuse to visit Georgetown. I couldn't wait until classes ended so I could hustle to my favorite eatery, catch an avant-garde movie, or go shopping.

The bottom line was that I lost track of my original purpose for teaching the classes. And guess what? I lost my passion and drive. Predictably, my effectiveness plummeted, the feedback turned lukewarm, and student enrollment dropped. The possibility for greatness was slipping through my fingers.

At first, I was perplexed. What happened? What was going on? What could possibly account for this dramatic change in fortune?

With these questions in my mind, I quickly figured out the source of the problem. Getting back to basics, I asked myself these key questions: Why am I teaching these classes? What is my purpose for spending big chunks of my limited time on this earth to do this work? What is the real worth or value of leaving my family and spending days on end with these students?

Asked this way, the answer became obvious. I redirected myself to the original purpose of these classes: to profoundly contribute to the lives of the people who attended my classes. Once I did this, my enthusiasm rekindled, my effectiveness shot back up, and the participants' feedback again flew off the charts. The stars were again aligned in the heavens.

But, there was more. The more long-term benefit of this roller-coaster ride was that I went on a quest to articulate for myself my personal purpose in life. Why am I here? What am I on this earth to do? How can I capitalize on the answer to the questions I posed about my UVa work for my life as a whole? Once I thought through these questions and figured my life's purpose, the rewards started rolling in. Finding this purpose keeps me alert to the opportunities that exist each and every day to express it both in my professional and private life. Connecting to my purpose is what I do to keep my drive, dedication, and determination high and my effort unrelenting. Maybe as important as anything, my satisfaction stays jacked up most of the time because most of everything I do each day feels meaningful. So it can be for anyone.

THE THREE LEVELS TO WORK

To put all this into context, think of there being three levels to work. See which one typifies you, whether you are a helping professional, someone receiving guidance from a coach, consultant, or clinician, or just an individual working through this book on your own.

Level 1: A Job

A job can be anything from blue-collar labor to engaging in some white-collar profession such as brain surgery. The key to this level of work is that one views what one does as primarily a means to make a living – to put food on the table, to pay the bills, to save for retirement. Work, in other words, is a means to some practical end. One can easily change jobs when something better comes along because there is neither personal identification with nor deep satisfaction from it.

It is my observation that most people work at Level 1. There is nothing wrong with this. In fact, it is honorable to work to meet one's responsibilities. But, how much satisfaction does one get from one's work at this level? Typically, not a whole lot. How much drive, dedication, and determination would there be when one sees work as just a job? Obviously very little. What is the potential for producing great results? Virtually none.

Level 2: A Career

When one sees one's work as a career, one labels oneself as something. At this level, I, for example, would label myself as an organizational consultant, a clinical psychologist, or a teacher. When work is seen as a career, one sees oneself as part of something beyond oneself. So, the motivation to gratify one's sense of self, to create a positive reputation in one's field, to belong to a fraternity of colleagues, added to making a living, further stimulates one's drive.

When working at Level 2, it becomes difficult to switch careers. After all, there typically is a large amount of time, education, and money devoted to establishing oneself, not to mention the fact that one's identity is typically intertwined with what one does. Predictably, productivity and satisfaction are greater at Level 2 than at Level 1 – assuming, of course, that one has made a wise career choice. But rarely is one infected with Unrelenting Drive, Dedication, and Determination.

Level 3: An Expression of Passionate Purpose

To work at this level is rare, but it is the source of Unrelenting Drive, Dedication, and Determination. Why? Because most people long to engage in something that has deep personal meaning to them. They want their work to be about more than simply completing projects, winning cases, making money, beating sales goals, or solidifying one's self-esteem.

Henry Ford once said, "The whole secret of a successful life is to find out what it is one is to do, and then do it" (Ford, n.d.). The person working at Level 3 first has a clear conception of the burning "why" of his or her existence. Then this person intentionally expresses this purpose through his or her work (and ideally through every other arena of life as well).

Having this clear connection between your life's purpose and your work, you will reap the benefits. You will find meaning and experience passion each and every day. You will be dedicated and determined. You will very likely create the extraordinary results you want. And you will feel deeply satisfied, rewarded, and fulfilled in the process. After all, what you do for a living has passionate meaning to you.

THREE EXAMPLES OF WORK AS AN EXPRESSION OF PASSIONATE PURPOSE

My Mother

I am almost certain that my mom did not consciously think through a formal statement of her life's purpose. Nor did she hold a salaried job once she married my dad. Yet she was crystal clear about the burning "why" of her life – to love and support her husband, to cherish and grow her children, and to nurture her extended family and friends. Within the privacy of her corner of the world, I can attest that she was a happy person who succeeded at the highest level.

Coach Mike Krzyzewski

Coach K, the basketball coach at Duke University, has won four NCAA championships and coached the USA to an Olympic gold medal. He is, by the way, the winningest coach in men's basketball history.

You might think Coach K's purpose is to win basketball games. It isn't. Listen to what he says about his purpose: "I am not a basketball coach. I am a leader who coaches basketball. I have three goals with all my players – to make them a good student, a good citizen, and a good person" (Krzyzewski, n.d.).

No wonder Coach K remains so driven after decades in the pressure cooker of big-time college basketball. He has a Passionate Purpose beyond basketball that he expresses through his coaching. This not only drives him to put in the long, hard hours of scouting, recruiting, and practicing, but it also serves to keep him enthusiastic about and fulfilled in his work.

Dr. Martin Luther King, Jr.

Perhaps there is no better example of the power of Passionate Purpose than Dr. Martin Luther King. This man, as much or more than anyone else who walked the face of this earth, stands as a beacon for working at Level 3.

The most compelling statement of Dr. King's purpose, a purpose he infused throughout the fabric of his life's work, is contained in his immortal August 28, 1963 "I Have A Dream" speech delivered in front of the Lincoln Memorial in Washington DC. It is brilliant from start to finish and should be read in its entirety to fully appreciate its power.

Nevertheless, look at the following sentence that conveys the clear, powerful, poetic expression of the Passionate Purpose of Dr. King's life and work: "I have a dream that one day this nation will rise up and live out the true meaning of its creed: 'We hold these truths to be self-evident: that all men are created equal'" (King, 1963). Dr. King's Passionate Purpose fueled the Unrelenting Drive, Dedication, and Determination that prompted him to devote each day of his life to make racial equality the rule, not the exception. Witness one more quote from the same "I Have A Dream" speech: "No, no, we are not satisfied, and we will not be satisfied until 'justice rolls down like waters, and righteousness like a mighty stream'" (King, 1963).

SELF-ASSESSMENT EXERCISE: LEVEL OF WORK

Positive change has to do with closing the gap between where one currently is and where one wants to be. This exercise can help you identify at what level you currently work. If you are not already working at Level 3, you can mindfully and purposely move yourself to Level 3 by doing the Passionate Purpose workshop to follow. I encourage you to do this self-assessment exercise with total honesty. It can serve as a springboard to doing what you already do at the same level of passion as my mom, Coach K, and Dr. King.

1. **At what level do I work?**

    _____

    _____

2. **What is my degree of drive, dedication, and determination at working at this level? Am I satisfied with this? Where would I like to be?**

    _____

    _____

3. **What is the quality of the results or successes I accomplish in working at this level? Am I satisfied with this?**

    _____

    _____

4. **What is the degree of satisfaction I derive from my level of work? Is this rewarding enough for me? How would I like to feel?**

    _____

    _____

5. **What would be the benefits to working at Level 3 . . .**

    . . . for myself? _____

    _____

    _____

. . . for my family? _____

_____

_____

. . . for my business, company, or institution? _____

_____

_____

. . . for my customers or clients? _____

_____

_____

. . . for my community? _____

_____

_____

Whether a helping professional or an independent reader, I hope you found this exercise enlightening. What did you learn from it? Is there a gap between where you are and where you'd like to be with regard to your passion, productivity, and satisfaction? If so, throw yourself into the Passionate Purpose workshop that follows.

THE PASSIONATE PURPOSE WORKSHOP

The Passionate Purpose workshop is a process of creating, not discovering. Discovering is about finding the life's purpose that is pre-determined for you; it is already there, and your responsibility is to figure out what it is. The problem with the discovery approach is that you have to take it on faith that you indeed have a pre-determined purpose. Furthermore, it can be disempowering in the sense that someone or something else defines your purpose; much like an arranged marriage, you think you must live it whether you like it or not. Most troublesome is that you can easily become discouraged and even self-deprecating if you fail to discover this pre-ordained purpose.

Creating, on the other hand, is about determining for yourself what your life's purpose is. There is no pre-determined purpose, nor is there a right or wrong one. It is what speaks to you, excites you, drives you. It is yours to create. It is for no one else, but in order for you to produce the great results you want in life.

The Passionate Purpose workshop is a four-step process modeled on Stephen Covey's Private Victory paradigm (1989): (1) reflect on your purpose; (2) create your purpose; (3) express your purpose throughout the fabric of your life; and (4) follow through, hopefully grounded on the paradigm of Unconditional Personal Responsibility.

I fervently urge you to take your time and devote energy and thought to this workshop. It made a tremendous impact on the productivity and pleasure of my life. It can for you as well.

Step One: Reflect on Your Passionate Purpose

With paper and pencil, thoughtfully reflect on the following five questions. They provide a basis for getting in touch with your deepest, most cherished values, pleasures, and desires. They can spawn the material for creating your life's purpose. For each, I will cite its source. I will also explain exactly how they are significant to developing your Passionate Purpose. And I will illustrate each from my own experiences to hopefully illuminate their relevance.

1.   What am I doing when I am in the flow?

"Flow" is a term coined by the eminent psychiatrist Mihaly Csikszentmihalyi, in his seminal book *Finding Flow* (1991). It refers to a state in which you are so focused that everything else but what you are doing disappears. Time seems to stand still. You are totally absorbed. What you are doing seems effortless and totally rewarding. When in the flow, you are most likely engaged in an activity that has deep personal significance to you.

I can identify three activities in my life in which I experienced flow. When I was younger, I played both high-school and college basketball, in fact playing on two NCAA Championship-winning teams. I remember being so absorbed playing the game that the spectators, the coaches, and to some extent the other players often seemed to disappear. I was aware of what was going on around me, of course, but my awareness was that of just playing basketball, with the court, the basketball, and even the other players pawns for empowered and creative expression. What a magical experience it was, though at the time I had no words to describe it.

In my current life, I frequently experience flow when doing psychotherapy with my clinical clients. Another flow experience is when I interact with workshop participants about some cogent issue of character or personality that I believe can spawn life-transforming performance and results. In these types of activities, I frequently become so absorbed that I completely lose track of time and wish the encounter would never end.

Becoming mindful of these flow experiences was very useful to me in creating my Passionate Purpose. Now is an opportunity for you to reflect on your own life experiences and identify times when you too were in the flow. Describe below three of these. What were you doing? What were you feeling? Most important, what was the meaning to you of what you were doing?

1. _____
_____
_____

2. _____
_____
_____

3. _____
_____
_____

2.   What is unique about me?

A number of years ago, I had become professionally frustrated and stale. I wanted to reinvigorate myself, but I was stuck as to what to do. I was unclear about what changes I needed to make. Wisely, I engaged a professional coach to help me break free of this logjam. Margaret lived in Colorado. We met by phone every ten days or so over the course of three months.

My breakthrough came when Margaret asked me a simple, but immediately unanswerable question: "What's unique about you?" This threw me. When I responded that I knew I had some talents, but that there was nothing I did that was unique to me, she emphatically said, "Nonsense. Until you clearly see your uniqueness, you will have a difficult time finding true professional satisfaction."

Boy, did Margaret throw me for a loop with those comments. She then assigned me the task of contacting five people who knew me well and asking them what they saw as my uniqueness. Being a dutiful student, I followed through. I emphasized to the five people I enrolled that the feedback I requested was not designed to stroke my ego: honesty and accuracy was what I wanted from them, whether what they had to say was positive or negative.

All five of the individuals I consulted provided quite valuable information. But one comment from my friend, Jim, was particularly helpful in my quest. He said, "You help make people's lives perfect, as they want it. You don't let them get stopped by their negative thinking. It's impossible to not play with you." In a million years I would never have been able to articulate that. I'm not sure I always succeed in doing what he described, but that indeed is the purpose behind everything I do. It captured my unstated purpose when I do psychotherapy, organizational consulting, and teaching. It opened the door to creating my Passionate Purpose. Ironically, it did not lead to major professional changes, but to a renewed appreciation of what I already did, along with some important tweaking.

I now urge you to uncover your uniqueness. Like me, I suggest that you enlist the observations and insights of trusted friends or colleagues. Take sufficient time to identify three to five people, contact them, and get their feedback as to what is unique about you. Write what they say:

Person 1: _____

_____

Person 2: _____

_____

Person 3: _____

_____

Person 4: _____

_____

Person 5: _____

_____

3.   About what am I enthusiastic?

Many people waste their time trying to fire themselves up. They invent all kinds of slogans and strategies to excite themselves into action. While this may work for a brief period, enthusiasm cannot be sustained through gimmickry.

The question now before you is: About what are you naturally enthusiastic? I, for example, am enthusiastic about helping my clinical clients and my business consultees defeat the problems they face and grow into all they can be. I also am enthusiastic about helping my sons develop strength of character. And I have enthusiasm for aiding and abetting my wife's happiness in life.

As you address this question, be careful to note that you may not be enthusiastic about some particular activity, but about the reason for doing it. I distinctly remember a housewife telling me she enthusiastically went about the onerous chore of cleaning her bathrooms. Seeing the incredulous look on my face, she explained that she saw this chore as an expression of taking loving care of her family.

Now reflect on your enthusiasms. What lights your fire? What turns you on? What do you care deeply about? The answers to these questions as well as what about them excites you will help you create your life's Passionate Purpose.

What I Am Doing When Excited   **Why It Excites Me**

_____   _____

_____   _____

4. **What could I do in life that would provide the most value, make the biggest contribution, and have the most positive impact?**

In helping people proactively take charge of their lives, Stephen Covey (1989) asks two profound questions:

1. What is one thing that, if you did it consistently and excellently, would make a profound, positive difference in your personal life?
2. What is one thing that, if you did it consistently and excellently, would make a profound, positive difference in your professional life?

My experience is that it takes people little time or effort to answer these questions. Following Covey, the next question to ask is: If you know these would make such a difference, why aren't you doing them?

Both the "what" and the "why not" questions are empowering. The "what" questions alert you to what exactly you need to do to produce great results. The "why not" question communicates that it is your responsibility to act to overcome the "reason" for not doing and make these results a reality.

Knowing what you could do that you are not doing but that would create magnificent results can deeply empower you. It can also help you create your Passionate Purpose. Now, please reflect on this question: What could you do that would have the most value, make the biggest contribution, and have the most positive impact in both your personal and professional life? To add meat to this question, make sure you note who would benefit and how. You? Your loved ones? Your friends and colleagues? Your clientele? Society at large?

In my personal life: _____

_____

_____

In my professional life: _____

_____

_____

5. What kind of person would I like to be?

To help you with this question, think of one or two people whom you most
admire and/or who have made the biggest impact on your life. What qualities
do they possess that made this impact?

When I asked myself this question, I was able to identify six people.
They included my mother and father; my English literature teacher in college,
Dr. Paul Grabel; my college basketball coach, Arad McCutchan; my psychology mentor, Dr. Albert Ellis; and my cousin, Bill Stocker. Each of these
cherished individuals possessed qualities that I deeply admired that I have
attempted to integrate into my character. They have helped give meaning to
my life.

I am sure that you can easily identify at least two significant people in your
life. Do so now, along with their notable qualities. This too can contribute to
you creating your Passionate Purpose.

	The Persons	**Their Notable Qualities**
1.	_____	_____
		_____
		_____
2.	_____	_____
		_____
		_____

Step Two: Create Your Passionate Purpose

Armed with all this introspective information, the second step in the Passionate
Purpose workshop is to create your Passionate Purpose. One of the mistakes
people often make is to rush themselves. Please do not do this. Reflect on your
answers to the five questions posed above. You might want to carry the answers
with you for a week or so and make additions or corrections as you go along.
You might also want to make notes about themes or phrases you want included
in your Passionate Purpose before creating it.

Your Passionate Purpose can be written in any format that communicates to
you. It can be a single phrase, a poem, a sentence, a brief paragraph, or even a

song or a picture. The point is that your Passionate Purpose must speak to you without concern for what others may think. It is meant to reflect your passion and spark your Unrelenting Drive, Dedication, and Determination.

I now offer you two examples. The first is that of Mahatma Gandhi and the second is mine.

Mahatma Gandhi

Let the first act of every morning be to make the following resolve for the day:

> I shall not fear anyone on earth.
> I shall only fear God.
> I shall not bear ill toward anyone.
> I shall not submit to injustice from anyone.
> I shall conquer untruth by truth.
> And, in resisting untruth, I shall put up with all suffering.
>   (Gandhi in Covey, 2008)

Dr. G.

To make a significant, positive impact on the health, happiness, and prosperity of myself, my loved ones, and the people with whom I work by being excellent in living, teaching, and modeling the principles of effective and joyful living.

You may relate to these two Passionate Purposes, or they may leave you cold. Regardless, note some of their features.

- They are stated positively.
- They are (relatively) brief.
- They include emotionally charged words.
- They represent a solid connection between their author's deepest values and their actions.
- They are written for the author, not anyone else.
- They provide a foundation for action.

Now it is time to create your Passionate Purpose. Remember to review the answers to your reflection questions and follow the guidelines above. Once you have penned a first draft, carry it with you for a week or two. Reflect on it. Make notes about changes you might make. After a week or two, compose your final version.

My Passionate Purpose

(First draft)

_____

_____

_____

_____

Step Three: Live Your Passionate Purpose

Now you have your Passionate Purpose in hand. While it hopefully inspires you, it is most likely too general to be of much practical value. To take it to the level of useful action, you need to plan exactly how you will express it throughout the fabric of your life.

Stephen Covey (1989) wisely suggests that the major roles we play in life can serve as vehicles through which to live out our Passionate Purpose. I, for example, took my Passionate Purpose and articulated how I would express it within the following four roles:

- myself
- husband and father
- external family
- career.

The question I asked myself was: How can I make a significant positive impact on the health, happiness, and prosperity of the person or people with regard to this role? With regard to work, I clearly articulated the opportunities to live out my Passionate Purpose with my clinical patients, my consultees, and the students in the courses, seminars, and workshops I conduct. In asking this question, I was surprised in that the answers stimulated me to create additional work activities that excited me even further and gave me additional opportunities to express my Passionate Purpose. I might also add that writing this book was one important way I discovered to live my Passionate Purpose through my work.

So, the next step in your Passionate Purpose workshop is to clearly articulate ways you can express your Passionate Purpose through each major role you play in your life. You can borrow my categories or articulate your own. By connecting what you do to this Passionate Purpose, how can your days not be filled with passion, drive, and satisfaction? How can you not be driven to act out your Passionate Purpose? How can you not create the extraordinary results you define significant?

My Roles	How I Can Express My Passionate Purpose
1. _____	_____
	_____
2. _____	_____
	_____
3. _____	_____
	_____
4. _____	_____
	_____
5. _____	_____
	_____

Step Four: Act Your Passionate Purpose Out

As discussed in Chapter 2, you must act with integrity by relentlessly following through on the action strategies that are an expression of your Passionate Purpose. With a commitment to your commitments, be sure to follow through, starting immediately.

INTENSIFIERS

Congratulations. By doing the Passionate Purpose workshop, you are now poised for producing great results in your life, however you define them. As a bonus, here are three additional tips to intensify the power of your Passionate Purpose. See if they don't deepen your passion in the pursuit of your great results.

One Day at a Time

A cornerstone of most all addiction recovery programs is to live one day at a time. This adage communicates that one need only choose not to indulge one's addiction until that day's bedtime. Sobriety is a less daunting challenge when applied to just today, rather than for the rest of one's life.

On a larger level, One Day at a Time also provides a philosophy by which to live one's life in general. It suggests that there are no guarantees in life, not even that one will be alive tomorrow. Therefore, one would be wise to passionately embrace what one has to do today. One's life can be much more vibrant, filled with so much more productivity, by focusing on the opportunities provided in one's life today. Concern yourself with tomorrow when it's here.

To intensify the power of your Passionate Purpose, you too can focus on One Day at a Time. Look at the day ahead and ask: What are the opportunities that exist today to express my Passionate Purpose – with regard to my work, my family, my friends, and myself? This will serve to connect your Passionate Purpose to your daily routine and make virtually every moment in your day meaningful and productive.

Adopt a Philosophy of Death

There is an old joke about a man strolling atop a 50-story building who trips and falls toward the pavement below. Passing the 27th floor, someone inside asks, "How's it going?" to which the man responds, "So far, so good."

The joke is that we all know what's coming: the pavement and death. Our death is probably the most sobering experience we face. One day we exist, the next we don't. No one wants to die, yet death is the destination we all share. No one has yet escaped it.

As daunting as our pending death is, it could very well be the single best invention for passion in life. Why? Because almost everything – our petty fears, our foolish pride, our immediate gratifications, our silly resentments – becomes virtually inconsequential in the face of death. Only what is truly important remains.

The bottom line is to remember that your time on Earth is limited. Remind yourself of this every day. Remember to live your Passionate Purpose – consciously, intentionally – each day. By doing this, you will increase your ability to get the most productivity and satisfaction possible out of each day of your life.

Check In Regularly

Life is filled with so many activities, chores, and responsibilities that it is difficult to stay focused on what is truly important. If not careful, our Passionate Purpose can be overridden by the mundane.

Regularly checking in on our Passionate Purpose helps to keep it front and center. I suggest that you adopt three specific practices that I have personally found useful. The first is to set aside a regular time to preview the upcoming week and note the opportunities that exist to live your Passionate Purpose. I do this each Sunday at about 6.00 p.m. The second is to begin each day with a preview of that day's activities and note the possibilities to fulfill your Passionate Purpose with regard to the events that are part of that day. The third is to spend a few minutes before important events to connect them to your Passionate Purpose. For example, I make it a habit before each class, seminar, or workshop I present to remind myself that this event is an important moment because it is an opportunity to make a significant contribution to people's lives.

AN ORGANIZATIONAL CASE STUDY

A number of years ago, the vice-president of a large metropolitan hospital called and asked, "Do you have a compassion workshop on your shelf?" She went on to explain that the Oncology Unit, the unit that provides medical care to people who are significantly ill with cancer, had received very negative feedback from their patients. It seemed that the unit scored very low on quarterly patient satisfaction scales, even getting write-in comments such as "We're not people to you, only bodies," "You herd us in and herd us out," and "You treat my disease but not me." With deep concern, she asked, "Can you help us?"

After reassuring her that I could indeed help, I went on to explain that compassion – the ability and willingness to understand and identify oneself with another person's inner experiences and to act accordingly – was not something teachable by traditional cognitive methods. I proposed, instead, that I devise a participatory process that would raise her staff's consciousness about the experiences and needs of the unit's patients. My goal was to help these medical professionals (doctors, nurses, aides, and technicians) raise their compassion quotient.

Process One was a straightforward warm-up in which I had the staff identify whom they were hired to serve. As expected, they identified the patients and patient families, but also added each other, various departments within the hospital, and the community at large.

Process Two was pivotal. After emphasizing that the view we hold of the core nature of people determines how we treat them, I provided these professionals with four metaphorical categories: (1) if we view people as a body, we focus on making them healthy and comfortable; (2) if we view people as a mind, we educate them; (3) if we view them as a heart, we provide them with warmth; (4) if we view people as a spirit, we help them experience their life as having meaning.

Armed with this model, I divided them into four groups and gave them this instruction: "Brainstorm everything you can think of that your patients and their loved ones want and need from you, putting each one under the proper heading – body, mind, heart, or spirit." I then sat back and held my breath.

Thankfully, these professionals delivered. Each group identified a number of things that their patients wanted and needed for their bodies and minds, but they identified a considerably larger, more profound list for their hearts and spirits.

There it was in black and white. While these patients certainly wanted competent medical care, they craved the human touch: caring and concern. Compassion mattered more to them than pills and procedures. As you can imagine, the data gathered from Process Two was more than a little eye opening, even prompting the unit administrator to say, "Wow, we spend 90% of our efforts on the body and the mind, but 90% of what our patients want is for the heart and the spirit." I am very happy to report that this process served the purpose of raising everyone's consciousness to the human needs of the people they served.

Process Three sealed the deal. In this process, I charged the unit to create an Oncology Unit Purpose Statement, which I reprint below. I want to emphasize that I purposely did not ever utter the word "compassion" to them. They arrived at this entirely on their own.

ONCOLOGY UNIT PURPOSE

We, the staff of the oncology unit, believe that all patients have a broad range of needs, all of which must be met. These include the nurturing of the body, mind, heart and soul.

FOR THE BODY: They need comfort, safety, and competent nursing care.
FOR THE MIND: They need specific, pertinent information communicated in terms that can be understood.
FOR THE HEART: They need acceptance, respect, compassion, encouragement, hope, honesty, and a sense of trust in their caregivers.
FOR THE SOUL: They may need the opportunity for spiritual and professional support in order to accept the present and prepare for the future.

Recognizing the extent and complexity of oncology patient needs, we acknowledge that we must combine professional **competency** with personal **compassion.** We therefore commit to the following standards to guide our actions and decisions.

COMPETENCY
WE WILL DEVELOP AND MAINTAIN:

- accurate technical skills
- an oncology-specific knowledge base
- physical assessment skills
- efficient time management
- teaching skills for patients, families, and the community
- consistent communications with all members of the healthcare team.

COMPASSION
WE WILL PROVIDE:

- empathetic support
- patient/family advocacy
- timely responses to patient requests

- active listening without judgment
- hope and encouragement
- assistance in achieving optimal quality of life
- honest communication with patients and their families.

Processes Four and Five served to integrate empathic compassion into the fabric of the unit's routines. In Process Four, the staff reviewed a typical day and identified those "moments of truth" when they had an opportunity to treat their patients with empathic compassion. Process Five directed them to find ways to make empathic compassion part of the Oncology Unit's culture. Some of the things they created included putting a framed copy of the unit's Passionate Purpose in every room in the unit; devoting one staff meeting a month to a discussion of the quality of their heart and soul behavior; and making these two ingredients a significant component of their hiring, promotion, and annual review processes.

The success of all this was confirmed shortly thereafter. The unit received off-the-chart marks in their very next quarterly review. More importantly, the staff sustained their excellent performance for the next two years. When my work with them ended, I had no doubt that they would continue to receive this fantastic feedback so long as they honored the Passionate Purpose they created.

In sum, every organization has a purpose – a reason – for its existence. This needs to be clearly articulated. Here are a few tips to make an organizational Passionate Purpose passionate and meaningful:

- Too often, upper leadership retreats to some posh location and creates the organization's Passionate Purpose in privacy. This is a big mistake. It is wise to involve everyone in the organization in its creation. Remember: more involvement at the beginning of a process leads to more buy-in at the latter part.
- Supplement the organization's Passionate Purpose with a set of Sacred Principles. The purpose tells the passionate "why" of the organization's existence, while the principles tell the sacred "how" people are to act in going about conducting themselves as they pursue their purpose.
- Regularly use the organization's Passionate Purpose. Too often, Passionate Purpose statements are put in expensive frames, mounted on walls, and then forgotten. They serve only as decoration. They should be used as a central feature in strategic planning, decision making, and problem solving.
- Keep the organization's Passionate Purpose alive. By this, I mean regularly discuss and frequently refer to the organization's Passionate Purpose. People forget it, get lost in their routine chores, and get caught

up in interpersonal turmoil. Keeping it alive can include, among many other things, discussions of its relevance and application at all staff meetings, as part of the explanation for why decisions are made, and its relevance to personnel matters.

- Integrate the Passionate Purpose into the fabric of the organization's processes, policies, and procedures. For example, the Passionate Purpose should be used as part of the hiring, promotion, and annual review processes.

A FINAL WORD

The theme of this chapter is that when we connect what we do to our Passionate Purpose in life, we cannot help but bring Unrelenting Drive, Dedication, and Determination to what we do. We become passionate and we are unrelenting in our drive to produce the great results we want.

The power of Passionate Purpose does not just apply to our work life. It applies to our relationship with our significant other, our role as a parent, our friendships, our avocations, and anything else in our life we deem important. The possibility for greatness, however you define it, is there for you if you infuse the fabric of your life with Passionate Purpose. Step up and do it.

REFERENCES AND SUGGESTED READING

Csikszentmihalyi, M. (1991). *Finding flow*. New York: Basic Books.

Covey, S. R. (1989). *The 7 habits of highly effective people*. New York: Simon & Schuster.

Covey, S. R. (2008). "The mission statement that changed the world." *Stephen R. Covey*. Available at: www.stephencovey.com/blog/?p=14 (accessed November 16, 2016).

Ford, H. (1922). *My life and work*. New York: Snowball Press.

Ford, H. (n.d.). Available at: www.azquotes.com/quote_369578 (accessed October 13, 2016).

Johnson, R. L. (2006). *Gandhi's experiments with truth: Essential writing by and about Mahatma Gandhi*. Washington DC: Rowman & Littlefield.

Jones, P., & Kahaner, L. (1954). *Say it and live it: The 50 corporate mission statements that hit the mark*. New York: Doubleday.

King, M. L. (1963). "I have a dream." Available at www.americanrhetoric.com/speeches/mlkihaveadream.htm (accessed November 16, 2016).

Krzyzewski, M. (2006). *Beyond basketball: Coach K's keywords for success*. New York: Hachette.

Krzyzewski, M. (n.d.). *Coach K*. Available at: www.coachk.com (accessed November 16, 2016).

Warren, R. (2002). *The purpose driven life*. Grand Rapids, MI: Zondervan.

CHAPTER 4

Fearlessness

Unlocking the door to boldness – freedom from ego

It is not the critic who counts, nor the man who points out how the strong man stumbled or where the doer of deeds could have done better. The credit belongs to the man who is actually in the arena; whose face is marred by dust and sweat and blood; who strives valiantly; who errs and comes up short again and again; who knows the great enthusiasms, the great devotions, and spends himself in a worthy cause; who, at the best, knows in the end the triumph of high achievement; and who at the worst, if he fails, at least fails while daring greatly, so that his place shall never be with those cold and timid souls who know neither victory nor defeat.

President Teddy Roosevelt

I invite you to thoughtfully read the above quote from the 26th president of the United States, Teddy Roosevelt. What an uplifting statement from a man who epitomized the fearless life. Especially note these phrases: "the man who is actually *in the arena* . . . who *strives valiantly*. . . .who knows the *great enthusiasms*, the *great devotions*, and *spends himself* in a worthy cause . . . who . . . if he fails . . . fails while *daring greatly*."

This is a wonderful ode to the potential for greatness that fearlessness offers. It captures the spirit of the firefighters who rush into burning buildings to save those trapped, the soldiers who serve our country on the front lines, and the ER doctors and nurses who rush to save the life of an accident victim. It illustrates the heart of the mother who dashes into traffic to pull her toddler to safety, the citizen who takes the microphone at a town hall meeting to voice his or her concerns, and the teenager who refuses to do drugs despite pressure from peers.

Those people display incredible acts of fearlessness, acts that prompt great results, sometimes in the sunshine of the public arena, other times in the anonymity of private life. So, we need to add the ingredient of Fearlessness to those of Unconditional Personal Responsibility and Passionate Purpose to produce the stew of Unrelenting Drive, Dedication, and Determination.

The purpose of this chapter, then, is to tackle the character trait of Fearlessness. As with Unconditional Personal Responsibility and Passionate Purpose, this trait is learnable, growable, and sustainable. Read on to discover the roots of Fearlessness, and then tackle the Fearlessness workshop and the Intensifiers that follow.

THE ANATOMY OF FEARLESSNESS

All you have to do is look around you to observe people who destroy their potential for great results because of fear. Consider the following four people whom I've had the privilege of treating:

- Fifty-year-old **Harriet**, a middle manager at a major insurance company, was so afraid of disappointing or angering anyone that she complied with any and all requests. As a result, she overworked herself to the point of exhaustion, reserved little time for herself or her husband, and finally became overwhelmed with stress. Coincidentally, she neglected for years to report multiple instances of sexual harassment acted upon her by her immediate supervisor.
- **Jack**, a hospital-based radiologist, was by all accounts an underachiever. He spent an inordinate amount of time reading X-rays, CT scans, and MRIs, all to make absolutely certain that he made no mistakes. The result was that he diagnosed fewer patients on average than his colleagues, regularly referred his more difficult cases to other physicians despite the fact that he had the ability to make the critical calls, and severely limited his and the unit's income. He consulted with me only after his supervisor threatened to let him go if he did not elevate his productivity.
- **Beth**, the co-owner of a struggling catering business, was very uncomfortable making sales calls on potential customers. What was even more debilitating was her difficulty in negotiating with her clientele, regularly giving in when challenged on price, menu, dates, and times. The topper was how easily she let her pushy, insensitive partner run over her.
- Seventeen-year-old **Brian** was the star guard on his high-school basketball team. Elevated to the varsity first string when only a wet-behind-the-ears freshman, he garnered all-conference honors in his sophomore year. Despite his noteworthy success, he reported a tremendous amount of anxiety before games and even before practices. The lid blew off during his junior year when he began to operate at three-quarter speed, with a corollary drop in almost all his productivity statistics.

It is fairly obvious that what choked these four people's ability to produce outstanding results was fear. They each shied away from competition, boldness, and risk-taking, acting in a risk-averse manner and focusing on avoiding errors, rather than going for the brass ring. They dedicated themselves to playing it safe

– that is, to setting easily attainable goals, putting aside their own desires, and working to be liked rather than to be successful. What they clearly needed was a healthy injection of Fearlessness to set them free.

The ABCs of Fear[1]

To understand what caused these people to feel fear, let me first take you through a stroll in the woods. Imagine you are camping in the wilderness. After a hearty breakfast, you go for a walk and run smack dab into a huge mama grizzly, trailed by her two cubs. Instantly, you recognize that you are in serious trouble, especially when she rises on her haunches, bares her teeth, and lets out a menacing roar.

Now, answer these two questions. First, how do you think you would feel? Second, what do you think you would do? If like me, you would most likely experience a great deal of fear, find your heart pounding uncontrollably, and either freeze in your tracks or run like the dickens. Right?

Now, let me get you out of the woods and back to civilization. Imagine you are faced with a challenge in your personal or work life, one in which you are not confident you can succeed and anticipate that someone may get upset with you if you fail. Let's say you are faced with making a presentation that will determine whether or not you'll land a huge contract for your company. Other possibilities might be meeting your future in-laws for the first time, or having to testify in court.

Choose any challenging situation you want and get it clear in your mind – see it, embrace it, feel it. Again answer the same two questions. How do you think you'd feel? How do you think you'd act? Not surprisingly, most people report that they would react pretty much the same in this situation as if they would when facing the bear – that is, with fear, physiological distress, and an urge to run away.

Decades of psychological lore have argued that fears are conditioned into us by our experiences. That is, we encounter some stressor, we experience fear, and, voilà, the fear response becomes connected or conditioned to the stressor. Then, when we come upon a similar stressor, it triggers the conditioned fear response.

However, while this may explain fear responses in a few cases, we have learned, through literally thousands of research studies, as well as hundreds of thousands of clinical cases, that this is not so for the majority of people. Following the ABC model[2] used by Rational Emotive Behavior Therapists (see Figure 4.1), we know that people literally think themselves (at B) into their fear (at C) about the adversities or challenges they face (at A).

To put flesh and blood on this model, let's go back to the woods. Most likely, when confronting the bear (the A), you thought (at B) something along these lines: "Oh my gosh, I could be killed. That would be horrible. I've gotta get away." Then, thinking along these catastrophic, life-or-death lines, you caused yourself to experience fear (the C).

Activating Event	Belief	Emotional Consequence
Activates	Causes	
A ⟶	B ⟶	C
– Past – Present – Future		– Fear – Anxiety – Panic

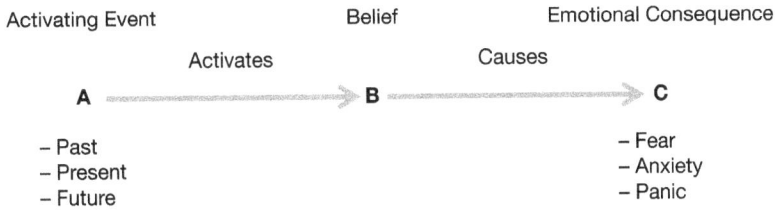

FIGURE 4.1   The ABCs of Fear

The point is that it was not the bear itself that caused your fear, but the way you thought about it. Though foolish, imagine thinking thusly at B: "How cute that bear is. I know she's friendly. I think I'll go rub her belly." As insane as that thinking would be, you wouldn't experience fear at C if you truly thought along these lines at B.

Now, let's take a look at the personal challenge in which you experienced fear (the C). I'll bet dollars to donuts that, in facing the possibility of failing and/or looking bad in the situation (the A), you thought (at B) pretty much the same about it as you did about the bear. That is, you thought something like the following: "I absolutely have to do well and look good. It would be horrible if I failed. What a loser I'd prove to be!"

Do you see the similarities? In both sets of thoughts, you appraised the situation as horrible catastrophes that must be avoided at all costs. So there are two critical lessons we can take away from these two scenarios:

1. We create our own fear when we convince ourselves that some hardship, hassle, or setback is a veritable life-or-death horror, even when the reality is that it isn't. In other words, our catastrophic thinking creates our fear, not the onerous event itself. Once we construe in our mind that some hardship or hassle is a life-or-death situation, we cause ourselves to experience the same fear we'd have when facing the wrath of the bear. The bottom line: fear originates in our mind by how we mentally appraise the situation.
2. To become fearless, we need to take control of the way we think. We need to rid ourselves of our Fearlessness-killing beliefs and indoctrinate ourselves with more reasonable, rational ones. By doing this, we can become fearless.

Fearlessness-Killing Beliefs

While there are just about as many things people can fear as there are stars in the sky, there are three irrational beliefs that cause most all fears. The first leads to the second, and the second is often capped off by the third. Once we rid ourselves of these beliefs, we can become fearless.

1. **The Set-Up: Necessitizing.** "Necessitizing" means convincing ourselves that something we desire is absolutely, unequivocally necessary. Through the use of such words as "need," "must," "have to," and "got to," we convert, in our mind, something that is desirable or in our best interest into a veritable life-or-death necessity, as per:

    *   "Because I want to do this well and succeed on this task, *I have to!*"
    *   "Because I want your approval, *I need it!*"
    *   "Because I don't want to feel upset, *I must not!*"

    Notice that none of these desired outcomes – succeeding, garnering approval, being emotionally comfy – are indeed a necessity, for we can easily continue to live and be happy whether we secure them or not. But, once we convert them in our minds into something life or death, necessary, or needed, the possibility of failing or experiencing disapproval or emotional pain becomes filled with fear.

2. **The Build-Up: Catastrophizing.** A second killer of Fearlessness is when we blow the degree of badness about some undesirable outcome way out of proportion. Instead of thinking "It would be a shame," "How unfortunate," or even "That sucks" when confronted with adversity, we think:

    *   "It would be *horrible* if I fail to get this book published."
    *   "It would be *awful* if he doesn't like or respect me."
    *   "It would be *terrible* not to win this competition."

    Notice that catastrophizing rates the degree of badness of some potential adversity at or even over the top, from a hassle or a hardship to something virtually unbearable. Once we rate some negative outcome this dire, we scare ourselves to death about the possibility of it happening.

3. **The Final Blow: Ego.** Ego is perhaps the worst thing ever invented. It refers to the cognitive process of judging or evaluating one's total self as either good or bad, worthwhile or worthless, a success or a failure. Instead of just accepting ourselves as alive and human, holding ourselves unconditionally worthwhile simply because we exist, ego connects our worth to some internal quality (e.g., our looks, IQ, culinary skills) or to some external circumstances (e.g., our success, the approval of others, the success of our children).

    Thus, by thinking that our worth is dependent on either doing well or looking good, every day poses many threats. For, if we connect our worth to doing well on a certain thing, such as the success of today's luncheon presentation at the Rotary Club, then we had damn well better do well to prevent the loss of our immortal soul. If we think we are only worthwhile if someone likes us, then we will automatically think of ourselves as worthless if not. Pretty serious stuff, and inevitably frightening, because, by failing, we are in danger of becoming a totally, thoroughly worthless being.

To put these three Fearlessness-killing beliefs together, let's revisit the fearsome foursome. Imagine you could read their minds. Wouldn't their thinking sound something like the following?

Harriet: In order to be a *worthwhile person*, I *must* have people like and respect me. For anyone to be frustrated with or disappointed in me is so *terrible* I absolutely couldn't bear it.

Jack: I *must* do well and never make a mistake. It would be *horrible* to miss even one diagnosis, especially if one of my colleagues finds out. I would be *a sham* as a radiologist and a *failure* as a person.

Beth: It would be absolutely *awful* if somebody ever got upset with me. I *must* never have that happen, as I would just *hate myself*.

Brian: What *gives me worth* is my basketball ability. I therefore *have to* do well or else I'm a *failure*. It would be just *horrible* to ever be bested.

Both research and clinical experience tells us that these three beliefs indeed prompt human fear. Furthermore, they are reciprocal and synergistic. For, if we truly must do well and be approved, then it follows that it is horrible to fail and that we are a failure. Reciprocally, if we would become a horrible failure if we don't do well or impress others, then it follows that we must do well. The bottom line: these beliefs kill the bold, no-holds-barred action that leads to producing extraordinary results.

The Fearlessness Formula

People who display Fearlessness are no different than their anxiety-ridden counterparts except in one critical respect: they deeply endorse and regularly act on the following rational beliefs. These are the opposite of the fearful ones already presented: necessitizing, catastrophizing, and ego. Study them carefully for they are beliefs to develop through the Fearlessness workshop to follow.

Not Life or Death

Fearless people clearly and repeatedly make the distinction between what they want, desire, or prefer and what are life-or-death necessities. I might, for example, want chocolate ice cream, but I certainly do not need chocolate ice cream. Why? Because, as much as I might like chocolate ice cream, I won't die without it. I don't need it.

This distinction is easy enough to make when applied to ice cream, but not so easy when applied to more important issues, like success and approval. But, if you think about it, the distinction still holds. Though you may think you need to succeed at that business, get into that college, or be loved by that significant other, these outcomes in truth are only desirable, not necessary. You may be deprived, frustrated, and saddened, but you will not die if you do not produce these results. Life will indeed go on with the myriad possibilities for success and happiness that still exist despite not getting what you want.

With regard to Fearlessness, once you stubbornly refuse to cross the divide between a desire and a necessity, you preclude the possibility of the fear that blocks full-bore, Unrelenting Drive, Dedication, and Determination. Revisiting the high-school basketball player Brian, imagine how fearless he will be on the court once he trains himself to think along the following lines:

> I really want to do well and succeed on the court. Why? Because I get so much pleasure from it. Heck, I might even get a free ride through college. But, it's only desirable, not an absolute necessity. Moreover, there is more to me than basketball, and I can still have a happy life even if I'm not God's gift to the hardwood.

Note that Brian's new self-talk is both realistic and freeing. If our friends Harriet, Jack, and Beth also adopted similar lines of thinking, they too would be freed to fearlessly pursue their own version of greatness.

Perspective

Fearless people not only refuse to necessitize, they also don't catastrophize. They make sure to think of the bad things that could happen to them as only as bad as they really are – no worse.

Whether in my clinical, consulting, or coaching role, I teach people to use what I call the Badness Scale to build perspective. Anything and everything that could go wrong in life can be placed somewhere between 1% and 100% bad on this scale. Only a few things rise to the level of 90% bad or higher. A mother might place the death of her four-year-old daughter at this level. Another person might rate all his loved ones being killed in a plane crash right up there. We might think of 9/11 at the 90% or higher level. Nevertheless, thinking about it realistically, a good 99% of the bad things that happen in life fall into the 1–10% bad range, whereas very few things rise into the 90% bad or worse.

The unfortunate thing is that people so often rate things so much higher on the Badness Scale than they really are, thereby scaring themselves into inaction. The value of this scale is that it can help people see their potential misfortunes in the proper perspective, the result being that they do not create in themselves the fear that blocks bold action.

Imagine overhearing the following conversation with Beth, the caterer:

Dr. G.:   So, Beth, let's say you stuck to your guns and refuse to lower your prices for a customer. What's the worst thing that would happen if you did that?

Beth: I'd lose the sale.

Dr. G.:   OK, so, on the scale, from 1 to 100, how bad would that rate?

Beth: A 50.

Dr. G.:   Really? As bad as a heart attack, your house burning down, your husband suffering a stroke?

Beth: I guess not that bad.

Dr. G.:   Think like a scientist for a minute, without emotion – rigorous and exact and realistic. Give me an accurate reading.

Beth: Maybe 10%.

Dr. G.:   There you go. It's really way down at the bottom of the scale, isn't it? Nobody dies, there are tons of other customers, and you still have your skills even if this one customer doesn't appreciate you. Isn't that true?

Beth: You're right. When I think about it, it's just a bump in the road, not like going off a cliff to my death.

Dr. G.:   Exactly! And if you thought about it like that, would you feel so scared and intimidated?

Beth: Not at all.

Dr. G.:   And you'd stand up for yourself, wouldn't you? Now, it's our job to get you to think realistically, in perspective like this, all the time. Then you'll soar.

Unconditional Self-Acceptance (USA)

The existential philosopher Jean-Paul Sartre (1943) brilliantly described what he called the Cycle of Life (illustrated in Figure 4.2). The cycle begins at the first moment of life. At birth, we have Being or Self. If the infant at this young age had the ability to speak, he or she would simply say, "I am."

Going forward, from Being comes Doing. Early on, the infant's doings are rather primitive (e.g., sleeping, sucking, swallowing), but his or her doings gradually become more and more complex over time, including, for instance, thinking abstractly, acting with purpose, and feeling deep, profound emotions. Then, from

Being   ⟶   Doing   ⟶   Having
(I am)   (I do)   (I have)

FIGURE 4.2   The Cycle of Life

Doing comes Having in that, by doing, a person ends up acquiring all sorts of "haves" – a multitude of personality and character traits, various physical features, a job, a career, friends, enemies, a house, social roles, a car, and on and on.

According to Sartre, this is the natural, normal progression. We begin life with Being, then from Being comes Doing, followed finally by Having. He claims that this cycle is one-way and irreversible (Sartre, 1943).

Grave problems arise, Sartre goes on, when we pervert the Cycle of Life – that is, when we reverse the cycle by defining our Being, our Self, by what we do or have. A common example is when we define our Self or Being by our career, such as "I am a psychologist," by some major role we play in life, such as "I am a mother," by some attribute we possess, such as "I am a kind person," or by some achievement, such as "I am a success."

Sartre notes that when we fall into this perversion, we put ourselves at risk in two major ways. First, when we define our Being by our Doing or Having, we effectively box ourselves into that identity, making it difficult if not impossible to operate outside this definition. If, in my view, for example, I am a psychologist, how in the world could I possibly choose to give up doing psychology for that would mean, to me, I'd lose my Being, or my Self? As a result, we lose the freedom to change course.

Sartre tells us that the second risk to this perversion is despair. Take, for example, the mother who falls into a deep depression when her child leaves home to go to college. This mother experiences what has been called "the empty nest syndrome," not just because she misses her daughter, but because, in her eyes, she has lost her Self and thus her reason for living.

But, if I may be so bold, I want to go one step further than Sartre. An even worse perversion beyond defining our Being by our Doing or Having is to rate, judge, evaluate, or esteem our Being as good or bad by how well we Do or Have. Thus, once I perversely define my Self as a psychologist, I then will easily rate my Self as good or bad, depending on whether I do well or poorly in practicing psychology.

By virtue of this second perversion, I have in effect invented my ego (good or bad) and created my self-esteem (high or low). Now, I have put myself in a no-win, fearful situation: if I already esteem my Self as bad, worthless, or a failure, I will be chronically fearful about undertaking future efforts for they may re-affirm my Self's worthlessness; but if I currently esteem my Self as good, I will still be fearful because it is always possible to fail and therefore transform into a worthless Being.

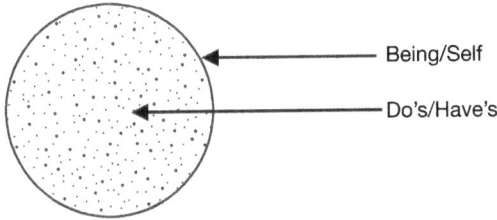

FIGURE 4.3   Unconditional Self-Acceptance

Thankfully, we have an antidote: what the renowned psychologist Dr. Albert Ellis called Unconditional Self-Acceptance (USA) (Ellis, 1977). As in Figure 4.3, think of your Self or Being to be the circle, and everything you Do or Have represented by a dot in the circle.

Your circle (Self) contains millions of dots, each representing a discrete action (a Do) or a discrete personal characteristic, a role, or a tangible possession (a Have). You may succeed wildly or fail miserably at one of these dots, but there is no logical or empirical way to generalize from any one dot to the whole of your total Self or Being. You may aggrandize any trait or performance ("That was wonderful what I did") without aggrandizing your Self ("I'm a wonderful person"). Likewise, you may damn some trait or performance ("That sucked") without damning your Self (e.g., "I'm a rotten person").

So, Unconditional Self-Acceptance means you first give up Self defining; to you, you just are, as opposed to being a something – i.e., a psychologist. Second, since you do not define your Self, you also give up Self judging, rating, or esteeming. The grand result is that, with the risk of Self off the table, you take the existential fear of failure or rejection away as well.

Imagine how fearless Harriet would become by shifting her thinking to "Well, I might indeed act badly and fail with this person, but this one failure hardly generalizes to my whole Self to make me a total failure." Similarly, picture Jack thinking, "I sure don't want to ever misdiagnose a patient, but even if I do, that hardly means I'm a totally terrible radiologist, much less a worthless person." No Self, no fear! No Self rating, no fear! No Self judging, no fear!

THE FEARLESSNESS WORKSHOP

Modern lore teaches us that Fearlessness is a capacity some are fortunate to be born with. You either have it or you don't. You're either John Wayne or Casper Milquetoast. If you think of Fearlessness as a trait firmly established by the luck of birth, you run the risk of passively accepting fear as your lot. You then are less likely to act to overcome your fears in order to be able to create your great results.

But we are all made up of the same DNA. It is more accurate to think of Fearlessness as a muscle that may be weak, but that can be strengthened. All we have to do is exercise it and then maintain it. In the Fearlessness workshop, I will take you through the five steps to build your Fearlessness muscle. If you avidly repeat the steps each day for the next couple of months, you will find your fears falling away, as have untold number of others.

A word of caution: disabling fear-making beliefs and adopting Fearlessness ones is difficult. If you are a layperson, take your time and really reflect on each step. Better yet, enlist a therapist, consultant, or coach to help you. If you are a helping professional, be sure to take an active role in guiding your client through this workshop.

Step One: Identify Your Fear

Any growth process starts with an awareness of where you presently are. It is therefore wise for you to be fully alert to situations in which you experience fear, as these are opportunities to beef up your Fearlessness muscle. Review your life and note below situations about which you find yourself fearful. These situations can involve people, places, or circumstances. Then note exactly what it is you fear in these situations (e.g., failure, rejection, disapproval, discomfort).

Fear Situation   **What I Fear**

1. _____   _____

                                                   _____

2. _____   _____

                                                   _____

3. _____   _____

                                                   _____

4. _____   _____

                                                   _____

5. _____   _____

                                                   _____

Now, whenever you actually face or know you will face these situations, you can view these as opportunities to build your Fearlessness muscle by using the next four steps. Just as you need to repeatedly do those curls to strengthen your biceps, you will need to repeatedly do this mental lifting.

Step Two: Track Down Your Fear-Making Beliefs

Do not forget that you cause your own fear by your necessitizing, catastrophizing, and/or Self-rating beliefs. This is truly good news; if facing the possibility of failing could actually cause you to experience action-crushing fear, you would be helpless but to experience it.

So the second step in your Fearlessness workshop is to bring into conscious awareness those beliefs you hold that drive you to be fearful. Repeatedly doing this step will help you in two ways. First, by identifying the specific beliefs that cause you fear, you can divest them of power through Steps Three, Four, and Five. Second, it will gradually raise your ability to quickly identify these fear-producing beliefs so that, after a while, you can catch and replace them on the fly.

Taking the fear situations you identified in Step One, track down your fear-creating beliefs. Hint: as with the examples of Harriet, Jack, Beth, and Brian on page 53, look for your necessitizing (e.g., "I must, have got to, have to, or need to do well and look good"), your catastrophizing (e.g., "It would be awful, horrible or terrible to not do well and look bad"), and your Self-rating beliefs (e.g., "If I fail at that, then I'm a failure"). Be sure to write out these beliefs in sentence form.

Fear Situation	Fear-Producing Belief
1. _____	_____
	_____
2. _____	_____
	_____
3. _____	_____
	_____
4. _____	_____
	_____
5. _____	_____
	_____

If you are like the hundreds of thousands of people who have conquered their fears, you will notice the themes of necessitizing, catastrophizing, and Self rating repeating themselves over and over. This is because they have become so ingrained that you automatically think them. It is good for you to become aware of these as you can go to Step Three in which you begin to erase them from your thinking.

Step Three: Destroy Your Fearful Beliefs

The purpose of Step Three is to critically analyze the validity of your fear-producing beliefs so that you can clearly see how incorrect they are. What you do is take each of these beliefs and energetically dispute them until you reveal to yourself how absurd and self-defeating they are. Repeatedly doing this over time will break their grip on you.

To dispute your fear-producing beliefs, you can use the Socratic method by asking and answering the following two questions, each of which has a follow-up question. Note that they stimulate you to logically and empirically think through your beliefs to provide reality-based, rational answers.

1. Is the belief true or valid? Why not?
2. Does this belief help or hinder my ability to produce my great results? How so?

In order to help you dispute your fear-producing beliefs, I offer you a few cogent arguments against necessitizing, catastrophizing, and ego. As you do your disputation below, you can use these as a crib sheet.

Disputing Necessitizing:

- This is not life or death; it is only a preference, something desirable or beneficial, as opposed to something that is absolutely necessary for existence.
- This is perfectionistic in that I am telling myself I must always do well and be approved. Everybody who has ever lived has at times failed at something and garnered the disapproval of others. I am not God, nor am I an exception to human imperfection.
- I am being illogical in thinking that, just because it is valid for me to want to succeed and look good, it follows that I must, need to, or have to. That conclusion does not follow from the premise.
- To think that I must succeed is grandiose and infantile because I am putting myself at the center of the universe. Like a two-year-old having a temper tantrum, I'm thinking that, because I want something, I have to succeed at getting it.
- It is debilitating and self-defeating to think this way because it causes me fear and easily prompts me to avoid the sustained effort I need to achieve the great results I want.

Disputing Catastrophizing:

- Thinking some setback to be awful, horrible, or terrible blows the degree of badness way out of proportion. With the death of everybody I love being 99% bad, this failure hardly rises anywhere close to that level. The truth is that this potential setback is just a hardship or hassle, not a horror.

- The loss of this valued outcome hardly takes away everything else that is good in my life; that is, while I indeed have this hardship, I still have my family, friends, job, home, interests, and health, so all and everything in my life is not lost by this one possible setback.

- Despite this adversity, I still have my future and every possibility to create what I desire so long as I am willing to devote the necessary time and energy to making it happen. In other words, failing at this endeavor hardly takes away all the results I can experience as I move forward in life.

- While certainly undesirable and disappointing, I surely can stand this failure or setback. As Nietzsche noted, what doesn't kill me can make me stronger.

- To view some failure or disapproval as a catastrophe will only serve to scare me away from strong, bold, no-holds-barred effort. In turn, that avoidance will certainly limit, if not destroy, the possibility for me to produce my great results.

Disputing Ego:

- When I rate, judge, or esteem my whole Being as good or bad, I generalize from one performance or quality (a Do or Have) to my whole Self. This is a gross overgeneralization in that I make myself totally, 100% this one thing.

- Once I totally rate my Self as all good or all bad, I freeze myself in time such that I become this Being forever. This precludes, at least in my mind, the possibility for future change.

- By labeling my Self a failure as a result of failing at some particular effort, I can easily conclude I deserve no good in life. I thereby become vastly demotivated and thus unlikely to persist until I succeed to get the results I want.

- By thinking about my Self negatively, I easily lose confidence in my ability to succeed in future efforts.

- I live in fear and passivity, states counter to bold action. For, if I judge my Self a failure, I am always in danger of reaffirming it.

Armed with these arguments, dispute each of your fear-producing beliefs in turn. Take your time, thoughtfully think them through, and show yourself how foolish they really are. Remember: you will need to do this daily for a while until you deeply internalize the absurdity of your fear-producing thinking.

My fear-producing belief: _____

_____

_____

_____

Is this belief true or valid? Why? _____

_____

_____

_____

Does this belief help or hinder me? How so? _____

_____

_____

_____

Step Four: Reformulate Your Fearlessness Beliefs

The first three steps of the Fearlessness workshop help you to acquire necessary insights – where and when you have fear, exactly what are your fear-creating beliefs, and the understanding that these beliefs are anti-empirical, illogical, and self-defeating. Step Four helps you to adopt new rational beliefs that open the door to Fearlessness.

For each of the fear situations you noted in Step One, write a new belief that counters your fear-creating ones. Hint: be sure to formulate beliefs that are not life or death (e.g., "I'd like to do well in this, but I don't have to"), that show perspective (e.g., "It would be disappointing to fail in this, but it's hardly the end of the world"), and that convey Unconditional Self-Acceptance (e.g., "I sure as heck can't become a total failure even if I do poorly in this one thing").

Fear Situation	Fearless Belief
1. _____	_____
	_____
2. _____	_____
	_____
3. _____	_____
	_____
4. _____	_____
	_____
5. _____	_____
	_____

Step Five: Act With Fearlessness

To deeply ingrain your new fearless beliefs, it is important for you to also act boldly. To mentally argue against your fearful beliefs in Step Three, while still acting as if they are true, will lead you nowhere.

For each of your fear situations, write the actions that would not only help you ingrain Fearlessness beliefs, but would also lead you to create the great results you want.

Fear Situation	Fearless Action
1. _____	_____
	_____
2. _____	_____
	_____
3. _____	_____
	_____
4. _____	_____
	_____
5. _____	_____
	_____

Great job. Now, eradicating any bad habit takes both time and elbow grease. To become fearless in the pursuit of your great results, I strongly urge you to build the following two activities into your daily routine. First, reserve 20–30 minutes each day for doing the Fearlessness workshop on some fearful circumstance in your life. It is okay if you use the same event many times, for it is changing the belief we are after, not the event per se. After a month or two, you will start seeing the change. Second, be alert to moments in which you experience fear during your day. When you find yourself fearful, instantly track down the inner necessitizing, catastrophizing, and/or Self rating that drive your fear (Step Two), dispute them on the spot (Step Three), and immediately replace them (Step Four). Then act fearlessly (Step Five). These are opportunities not to be missed.

INTENSIFIERS

What follows are three strategies you can use to intensify your Fearlessness. Regularly exercising these will help you become more and more bold in the pursuit of your greatness.

Think Breakthrough, Not Breakdown

Somewhere along the line, most of us have taken a wrong turn with regard to how we have viewed mistakes and failures. When learning to walk, talk, and ride a bicycle, we failed a hundred times before mastering the task, all without self-criticism or damning.

As we passed through childhood, though, most of us unfortunately embraced a whole different way of thinking. Perhaps because of biological tendencies, and most certainly the result of socialization experiences, little by little we adopted what has been called a breakdown mentality. That is, we learned to think that a mistake or a failure must never happen, that it is horrible when it does, and that someone (me? you? they?) needs to be blamed. Without meaning to, we developed fears of failure that block our willingness to take risks. This perspective gets reinforced all the way to the grave.

A better way to approach life is what is called the breakthrough mentality. In this, there are no mistakes or failures except by definition. A mistake or failure only exists because you label it as such. Thomas Edison wrote:

> It has been just so in all my inventions. The first step is intuition – and that comes with a burst. Then this gives out and then a little difficulties and faults show themselves and months of watching, study, and labor are requisite before commercial success – or failure – is certainly reached. (Shapiro, 2006, p. 226)

Every setback, then, is an opportunity for a breakthrough; it is an opportunity for new learning, for new possibility, for getting one step closer to success.

Taking a breakthrough mentality makes it difficult to experience fear. For no longer is failure a horror or a reason for self-flagellation. Rather, it is something to be taken advantage of along the path to success. The whole playing field thus changes.

Eliminate Critical People

An essential component of recovery from alcoholism is to eliminate the people who are part and parcel of the addiction. Doing this sometimes takes great courage and can result in some grief, but the alcoholic cannot afford to associate with enablers.

Similarly, to act with Fearlessness, you may find it necessary to weed out those people who champion necessitizing, catastrophizing, and especially Self rating. While probably not meaning to be, these people are toxic transmitters of the fear-producing bacteria.

Similarly, work hard to surround yourself with people who embrace life without fear. They are most likely people who think in terms of wants rather than necessities, dislikes rather than catastrophes, and failing rather than being a failure. They most likely go for the gold with enthusiasm, not trepidation. Hang out with them. Watch them. Model them.

Celebrate Your Good Qualities

You have two choices: you can focus on your faults and limitations or you can focus on your strengths and successes. While it would be foolhardy to ignore your weaknesses and mistakes, you would also be wise to be conscious of and acknowledge what you do well and what your good qualities are.

Don't be shy about this. Muhammad Ali famously said, "It ain't bragging if you can do it." You might place a small notepad next to your bed and each night before you go to sleep write down three to five correct things you did that day. Doing this will not only help you get into the habit of paying attention to your positives, but it will also serve to strengthen your Fearlessness.

AN ORGANIZATIONAL CASE STUDY

Several years ago, I presented an all-day leadership seminar sponsored by a Chamber of Commerce. Afterwards, one of the attendees, Rick, asked if we could chat. We sat the corner of the room and he complained that, despite his cajoling, pleading, and even threatening, he could not persuade the key people in his company to act outside their comfort zone and take any initiative on their own. He joked that he would pay me my weight in gold if I could transform his people into "a bunch of bold warriors."

How could I pass up such a challenge? I started my consultative efforts by conducting interviews with individuals from throughout the company. What I found was a pervasive fear of making mistakes and thus losing one's job. This fear came from two sources: (1) the weak economy, which prompted an overall worry about being downsized; (2) the persuasive fear that their hot-tempered owner, Rick, would impulsively ream out or even fire someone for blundering. In short, a play-it-safe attitude permeated the whole culture.

After completing the interviews, I sat with Rick and told him straight-arrow both my diagnosis and my prescription. I looked him in the eye and said, "You've lost your people's trust. They're afraid of you and of losing their job. What you're going to have to do is create a culture of Fearlessness that involves first you and then everyone else making big-time changes."

At first, Rick became defensive and debated me. But, I held my ground and slowly but surely convinced him of the accuracy of my message. Finally, he said, "OK, I'm in – how do we fix it?"

Here, in a nutshell, is what I did with this company, with Rick's full cooperation and involvement:

1. We first set up a company-wide meeting, with me at Rick's side, in which he summed up precisely what I told him was the problem and his role in it. He apologized for making their jobs so hard. He emphasized that, while he still expected standout performance, he valued each and every one of them and that he would commit to learn how to control his temper and gain back their trust.

2. This meeting set the stage for the cultural change effort. Using the ABC model of Rational Emotive Behavior Therapy (REBT), I coached Rick on how to relinquish the irrational beliefs that drove his anger and how to ingrain more rational ones that would help him keep his temper under control despite the inevitable mistakes his people would make. On each day I spent at his company, I reserved one hour to privately coach him, almost as if he were one of my patients in my clinical office.

3. Concurrently, I presented a series of Fearlessness workshops to all the employees of the company. In these seminars, I taught the ABC model, the irrational beliefs leading to fear, the disputation method, and the rational perspectives that would not lead to fear. I practiced them over and over in how to use the five-step process explained in this chapter's workshop and I emphasized the importance of acting boldly.

4. Those in leadership roles were taught coaching skills. The theme was that they, as leaders, had two major responsibilities: (1) to see to it that results are produced; (2) to continually grow the skillfulness of their people so that they gradually become more adept at producing expected results. I emphasized that mistakes and failures should be viewed as opportunities for coaching for growth. That is, good managers are hands-on managers, and hands-on managers conduct multiple coaching sessions each and every day.

5. With these major thrusts up and running, I kept up the assault on fear by helping them integrate the following into their company's leadership strategies:

    • Those in leadership roles, from the owner on down to the line supervisors, focused on catching direct reports doing good and praising them for it. Too many leaders fall into the criticism trap. This is when they expect employees to be perfect: when employees do well, they think that there is therefore no need for recognition; but, when there is a goof-up, criticism is felt to be justified. The result is that there is a preponderance of negative feedback that not only destroys goodwill, but also creates a fearful, timid approach to one's tasks in the workforce.

    • Those in leadership roles had to be exemplary models of Fearlessness. They had to walk the talk, openly acknowledging mistakes and failures, all the while communicating anti-necessitizing, anti-catastrophizing, and anti-judgmental messages.

- Those in leadership roles were told never to judge, damn, or negatively label anyone. It was okay to judge what people did, but never to judge their Being.
- The owner instituted a mistake of the month price. He gave a $100 gift certificate to the employee who made the biggest mistake that month, as determined by a majority vote of the entire employee body. The process was twofold: first, the employee had to nominate himself or herself, thereby serving to make mistake-making not to be feared; second, the employee had to have corrected and learned from the mistake. This opened the door for the workforce to not only acknowledge mistakes, but to constantly improve their work performance as well.
- Finally, those in leadership roles strove to give employees more and more freedom to make decisions. This communicated confidence, especially when they backed this up with praise for good decisions and coaching when mistakes were made.

It was a real pleasure consulting with this company. As the culture changed, the workforce became more bold and fearless. As the leadership saw this, they worked harder and harder to grow the culture. When I last saw them, they were a company of bold warriors.

A FINAL WORD

Along with Unconditional Personal Responsibility and Passionate Purpose, Fearlessness is a third pillar of producing great results. Not only does freedom from fear lead to peace of mind, but it also opens the door to the bold pursuit of one's dreams.

As with the two previous traits, Fearlessness is also a character trait. Like all character traits, it emanates from the mental perspective one takes – in this case, a perspective that holds virtually nothing as necessary, a catastrophe, or an indictment of one's Being or Self. This perspective is learnable and growable with the proper effort. It leads to bold risk-taking and no-holds-barred effort.

I encourage you to devote the time and effort it takes to rid yourself of your fearful ways of thinking. I've helped many hundreds of people do just that. I know you can and I know you will then be positioned to pursue your great goals.

NOTES

1. This section was co-created with my friend and colleague, Dr. Fred Fralick, for one of our leadership seminars.

2. Renowned clinical psychologist and founder of Rational Emotive Behavior Therapy Dr. Albert Ellis originally discovered these fear-producing beliefs, as well as the general outline of the Fearlessness workshop to follow.

REFERENCES AND SUGGESTED READING

Burns, D. D. (1993). *Ten days to self-esteem*. New York: William Morrow.

Carnegie, D. (1984). *How to stop worrying and start living*. New York: Simon & Schuster.

Ellis, A. (1977). "Psychotherapy and the value of a human being," in A. Ellis & R. Grieger (Eds.). *Handbook of rational-emotive therapy*. New York: Springer.

Ellis, A. (2000). *How to control your anxiety before it controls you*. New York: Kensington Publishing Corp.

Ellis, A. (2005). *The myth of self-esteem: How rational emotive behavior therapy can change your life forever*. Amherst, NY: Prometheus Books.

Hauck, P. A. (1991). *Overcoming the rating game: Beyond self-love – beyond self-esteem*. Louisville, KY: Westminster.

Roosevelt, T. (1910). Quote from speech titled "Citizen in a republic", delivered at the Sorbonne in Paris, France on April 23, 1910.

Sartre, J.-P. (1943). *Being and nothingness: An essay on phenomenological ontology*. New York: Washington Square Press.

Shapiro, F. R. (Ed.) (2006). *The Yale book of quotations*. New Haven, CT: Yale University Press.

CHAPTER 5

Interpersonal Intelligence

Building the strong relationships you need to
help you succeed – it starts with the heart

What you do is win with people.
Joe Gibbs, NFL Hall of Fame Coach

As I write this chapter, the bipartisan stalemate in the United States Congress rages on. While our country climbs toward being $20 trillion in debt, the immigration situation worsens, mass shootings happen all too often, the economy staggers at an anemic growth rate, and chaos in the Middle East becomes more and more dangerous, both Republicans and Democrats hold stubbornly to their rigid positions, unwilling and unable to cooperate to solve problems. What a mess.

What is going on in our nation's capital? Is it just politics as usual? Is it extremist party loyalty? Is it political ideology run amuck? Maybe it's a combination of all of these. But I think the problem goes much deeper. As I observe the depth of vitriol on both sides, with virtually no compassion or compromise, I suspect these problems represent a profound crisis in the heart and spirit of the men and women who are there to serve our country.

I remember years ago watching an interview with the actor Richard Gere. An avid Buddhist, he made the point that what's in your head determines to a very large degree how people respond to you. He illustrated this with a simple experiment he conducted in New York City before he became such a recognizable figure. He related that for two entire days, while walking the streets of this notoriously impersonal city, he would direct the thought, "I love you," to each person he passed on the street. Amazingly, without him smiling, nodding, or uttering a peep, Gere found that the New Yorkers he encountered began smiling at him as they passed.

This little story communicates wonders. It tells us that the attitudes we carry about people not only govern our actions toward them, but also influence how they respond to us. If we hold a loving, positive frame of mind toward people, we are likely to approach others with a spirit of kindness, generosity, and empathy, often stimulating that back in return. To the contrary, if we are negative or cynical in our attitude toward others, we will be dismissive or worse, thereby increasing the likelihood of receiving that back as well.

I think that what is needed from the people we elect to lead our nation is a fundamental transformation of heart and mind, a sort of interpersonal character transplant. Perhaps we should require all who aspire to elective office to provide us a résumé of how well they live by compassionate, intelligent interpersonal principles, in addition to their political postures and proposals.

What does all this have to do with Unrelenting Drive, Dedication, and Determination? "What you do is win with people," the former coach of the Washington Redskins, Joe Gibbs, tells us (Gibbs, 2002). The truth is that we live in an interdependent world, one in which we most often need the help of others to create the great results we covet. That is, we almost always accomplish much more with the enthusiastic support of others, as opposed to when we work alone or in conflict.

The evidence is overwhelming that people who achieve greatness are high in what I call Interpersonal Intelligence. By virtue of the perspectives they hold in their minds and hearts, they inspire loyalty, allegiance, and even devotion in the people they need in order to succeed. Witness what John Hancock, one of the original signatories of the Declaration of Independence, wrote to George Washington on behalf of the entire Congress after the general miraculously crossed the Delaware River and defeated the British troops at Trenton, New Jersey on Christmas Day, 1776:

> The victory at Trenton was all the more extraordinary given that it had been achieved by men broken by fatigue and ill-fortune. But troops properly inspired and animated by a just confidence in their leader will often exceed expectations, or the limits of possibility. As it is entirely to your wisdom and conduct, the United States are indebted for the late success of your arms. (McCullough, 2006, p. 284)

So, now we turn our attention to the character trait of Interpersonal Intelligence: what it is, its multiple ingredients, and how to grow it in yourself. It is one of the key secrets to creating greatness in life.

INTERPERSONAL INTELLIGENCE DEFINED

Let me start with an example. Brechenridge–Franklin Elementary School near downtown Louisville, Kentucky is a school that works. In this school, achievement is high, there is fervent student participation in classroom discussions, students act respectfully toward their teachers and work cooperatively in groups, and the classrooms function in a calm, orderly way with very few discipline problems.

The core of the Brechenridge–Franklin philosophy of education is captured in its CARE for Kids program. CARE stands for four principles: Community, Autonomy, Relationship, and Empowerment. In operation, it practices five fundamental strategies: (1) daily morning meetings in which important classroom decisions are made and discussions about salient topics take place (e.g., conflict resolution, bullying); (2) teachers and students jointly creating classroom behavioral expectations and consequences for violations; (3) direct teaching of social, emotional, and characterological skills, such as self-discipline and empathy; (4) teachers using precise language that directs the students to behave appropriately rather than words of criticism or judging; and (5) discipline that is geared toward growth rather than punishment.

CARE for Kids is the brainchild of the Jefferson County Public School's Superintendent Sheldon Berman, who sees social and emotional education as the key to academic success. Teachers in this school district must not only possess the ability to teach the 3 Rs, but they must also appreciate that CARE for Kids starts with their own inner values and principles. Much like Richard Gere, they must hold and project caring and respect.

Literary teacher Robben Seadler put it well:

> The better the relationship you have with the kids, the more they're going to want to learn, and the more they're going to take ownership of what you're to teach them. And when they feel that way, the behavior problems aren't there. (Rubenstein, n.d.)

Even deeper, teachers who implement CARE for Kids must make attitudinal shifts that come from the heart. Teacher Darren Atkinson captures this spirit when he says to his students, "I love each and every one of you. I may sometimes hate what you do, but I love you as a human being." He shared, "When these kids see and believe that you mean it, they want to work for you" (Rubenstein, n.d.)

As illustrated by the staff at Brechenridge–Franklin Elementary School, Interpersonal Intelligence is much more than simply a set of social skills. It is not just forcing oneself to practice good communication techniques, pasting a smile on one's face first thing in the morning, or partaking in jovial banter. Rather, Interpersonal Intelligence has to do with developing deep inner beliefs, perspectives, or paradigms that bubble warmth, caring, and even love toward others naturally from deep inside.

What follows are five traits that describe a person high in Interpersonal Intelligence: kindness, appreciation, Mutual Win, generosity, and empathic compassion. With diligence, each can be grown. As you read ahead, think of how developed you are in these traits. Then we'll tackle the Interpersonal Intelligence workshop.

Kindness

One of the most high-leverage things one can do to build trust, loyalty, and goodwill is to treat people with kindness. With most people, little things are big things. Every time we act in a kind way, we make a deposit in a person's goodwill account with us; every time we act in an unkind way, we make a withdrawal. The goal is always to be well in the black.

Motivational speaker John Parker Stewart presented in his excellent instructional video *Team of Champions* (1992) the case of a middle manager whose direct reports were willing to move mountains to help him succeed. He was a slight-built man, but large in Interpersonal Intelligence. A member of his team said of him, "He's a little guy, but he has these great big, long arms; he gives us emotional hugs each and every day."

Justice Potter Stuart once remarked, "I don't know how to define obscenity, but I know it when I see it" (Jacobellis vs. Ohio). Much like obscenity, kindness is hard to define in behavioral terms. People who possess the trait of kindness tend to act with consideration, sensitivity, caringness, thoughtfulness, and civility in interactions with others. We know it when we see it, but it's hard to concretize.

What is important to understand is that kindness is an organic concept, not a cookbookish set of to-dos. With this in mind, the following three mindsets spawn kindness. The deeper they are ingrained, the more likely we are to automatically treat people with kindness without the need to plan to do so.

1. **People are imperfect.** Remember that all people are intrinsically imperfect, fallible beings. They all have failings and shortcomings, and therefore will fairly frequently make mistakes. The issue is not whether they will, but when. All of us are always in the process of growing and changing, but never into a perfectly finished product.

   To treat people with kindness, we need to hold realistic expectations. Every last human being, ourselves included, is an FHB – a Fallible Human Being. We would be wise to keep this in mind so we expect them to err; when someone steps on our toes by acting foolhardily, we therefore practice tolerance, forgiving them even without the need for apology, and giving them the due respect they deserve despite their recent behavior.

2. **People are never to be judged.** Harkening back to Chapter 4, on Fearlessness, kindness also depends on separating what people do from who they are. Simply said, there are no all good or all bad people. We are all FHBs who variously do both good and bad. It is acceptable and even desirable at times to judge people's actions, but never to judge them as totally good or bad. This would be tantamount to throwing out a whole bushel of oranges because you found one of them to be rotten.

Mother Teresa once said, "If you judge people, you have no time to love them." So, kindness requires us to remove our judge's robe so we can open our hearts, even when our fellow humans are not at their best.

3. **People are thin-skinned.** Some wise person once remarked, "When you deal with the souls of men, take off your shoes because you walk on sacred ground." I would also suggest that you walk on tender ground. To act with kindness toward those we encounter, we must remember that everyone has soft spots or sensitivities; we are all tender of heart and ego. We must be aware that harshness, heavy handedness, or hardness can easily bruise.

Appreciation

My wife and I homeschooled our son throughout his school years. He did quite well, but in the beginning he threw up quite a bit of resistance. About once a week, Patti would call me at work, overwhelmed with frustration and discouragement, sometimes even in tears, because Gabriel fought her tooth-and-nail every step of the way. She was a saint to hang in like she did.

The stress and strain became such that we considered sending Gabriel to public school. But, before throwing in the towel, we decided to give it one more try, but this time with the addition of a formal appreciation system. Assessing that the problem was not Gabriel's intelligence but his self-discipline, we sat him down and told him the following:

> Gabriel, we know that you are smart and can do well. We also know that we are asking you to do things that are difficult for you in the beginning. To help you, we are going to show you our appreciation, not for mastering the subject, but for cooperating and working hard. You don't have to be perfect and not make mistakes; all you have to do is cooperate and work hard each day at school.

We then laid out the appreciation program, which consisted of three levels. First, if Gabriel cooperated at school that day, he would get a gold star, which would entitle him to a treat that evening (e.g., ice cream for dessert). Second, five gold stars for the week earned him a special outing with his dad on the weekend. And third, he earned a "big appreciation" for four consecutive weeks of five gold stars, such as an extra-special outing or a new PlayStation game.

All of this was time consuming and sometimes expensive, but it worked. Gabriel knocked himself out for the appreciation. Why? Because appreciation is one of the deepest longings of the human spirit.

Lest you think this is just a kid thing, let me share a charming tale from The Beatles, arguably the greatest and most beloved rock band of all time. It seems that during the recording of their legendary *White Album*, Ringo Starr decided to leave the band because he felt unappreciated. In his own words, he said, "I went to see John, who had been living in my apartment in Montague Square with Yoko since he moved out of Kenwood. I said: 'I'm leaving the group because I feel unloved and out of it'" (The Beatles, 2000, p. 311).

So, Ringo left The Beatles. How did it work out? Let's turn to the sage psychologist Paul McCartney to give us the answer:

> I think Ringo was always paranoid that he wasn't a great drummer. But, I think his feel and soul and the way he was rock solid with his tempo was a good attribute. You could just tell Ringo how it went and leave him – there was always this great noise and steady tempo coming from behind you. . . So at that time we had to reassure him that we did think he was great.
>
> That's what it's like in life. You go through life and you never stop and say, "Hey, you know what? I think you're great." You don't always tell your favorite drummer that he's your favorite drummer. Ringo felt insecure and he left, so we told him, "Look man, you are the best drummer in the world to us." He said, "Thank you," and I think he was pleased to hear it. We ordered millions of flowers and there was a big celebration to welcome him back to the studio. (The Beatles, 2000, pp. 311–12).

Appreciation works. It makes us feel significant and special. It gives us pleasure. If it is important to a world-famous person like Ringo Starr, adored by millions, it's surely important to us regular folk. And, of course, people don't separate us from the way we make them feel; they will be attracted to us if we make them feel appreciated, but they will get their adversarial energy stirred when attacked or ignored.

So, to enroll those we need to help us produce our great results, we need to regularly bathe them in the milk of our appreciation. But remember: showing appreciation cannot be a mechanical thing. If approached in this way, it will come across as phony. It has to come from the heart, backed by the following mindsets:

1. **Everybody values being appreciated.** Who doesn't puff up when made to feel appreciated? It's that hunger for appreciation that makes people feel good about and want to help the giver. It's that hunger for appreciation that, when not received, shuts a person down and drives them to greener pastures. Being mindful of this basic human craving primes you to be alert to opportunities to deliver heartfelt expressions of appreciation.

2. **Everyone has an occasional hard day.** No one is exempt from hardships and hassles. Sometimes, these frustrations are minor annoyances; at other times, they come from major setbacks. The point is that everybody struggles with life and indeed sometimes has a hard day.

Assuming that everyone we meet faces some struggle or another will help us be appreciative. It will help us to routinely be alert to opportunities to show our appreciation.

3. **Catch people doing good.** One of the most common killers of inter-personal goodwill is when we fall into what I called earlier in this book the criticism trap. This trap starts with the expectation that people will always do the right thing. Then, when they do, we don't bother to show appreciation because, after all, this was what was expected. But, when they don't, we critically let them know about it. The end result is that is that we end up being more critical than reinforcing, more negative than appreciative. What a killer of goodwill.

Developing the habit of showing appreciation to people starts with we ourselves appreciating how much our appreciation means to others. With this perspective, we will be surprised how many opportunities there are to show our appreciation. And we will reap the benefits in terms of loyalty, goodwill, and cooperation.

Mutual Win

I would be remiss if I did not include Mutual Win in a chapter on Interpersonal Intelligence. And it would be inconceivable for me not to give full credit to Stephen Covey, who brilliantly articulated this character principle in his seminal book *The 7 Habits of Highly Effective People* (1989).

It is important to emphasize that Mutual Win is not a communication technique nor a negotiation strategy meant to manipulate people. Rather, it is a frame of mind – a character trait – that guides one to conduct oneself in human interactions so that no one ever experiences defeat.

Mutual Win contrasts with two predominant mindsets in our society. The first is win–lose, where one is motivated to win or prevail out of a spirit of competition. The second is lose–win, where one defers or gives in out of a sense of being one-down. Mutual Win is a mindset in which one commits to strive for mutual satisfaction with all other people. It says that, since we live in an interdependent world where we most always need others to succeed, we will work in a cooperative fashion to forge agreements and resolve issues so that we both benefit. The ultimate expression is for a person to endorse the following way of thinking:

I am committed to finding a solution to any difference, disagreement, or conflict in all my human interactions in which there is Mutual Win and satisfaction. I won't settle for a solution in which another wins and I lose because I will feel bad. But I also won't settle for an outcome that ends up with me winning and someone else losing because they will end feeling bad. Ultimately we will both then lose. I will take responsibility for both of us winning.

I have observed the power of Mutual Win across the spectrum of my life experiences. As an organizational consultant, I have seen conflicted, entrenched business rivals, co-owners of businesses, departments within companies, and management and employees resolve long-standing, sometimes bitter disputes once they agreed to deal with each other from the Mutual Win perspective.

In my role as a clinical psychiatrist, I have worked with couples who harbored such animosity that they were on the brink of divorce. Those couples who were willing to embrace the spirit of Mutual Win almost always conquered their conflicts and salvaged their relationship. Those who persisted along the win–lose paradigm most often either parted ways or settled into a life of low-grade bitterness.

On a more personal level, whenever I have approached another with a Mutual Win mentality, my relationship with them has prospered. This has been true all the way from a contractor who built my house to my relationship with friends and neighbors. Perhaps most important, my wife and I have used this principle to successfully resolve three major disagreements. We are proud and happy that we had the Interpersonal Intelligence to do so as we each have been the beneficiaries.

Of course, people must possess solid communication, problem solving, and judgment skills to navigate to workable solutions amidst interpersonal conflict. Yet the key is the character paradigm of Mutual Win. There are three foundational mindsets you can adopt to help you intelligently relate with Mutual Win:

1. **There is plenty for everybody.** Most people hold a scarcity mentality. They think that there is not enough to go around. They therefore find it difficult to share, be generous, and root for another's success. The truth is that, in almost all situations, there is plenty for everybody – profit, customers, gadgets, whatever. The bottom line is that we can afford to seek mutual benefit.

2. **We live interdependently.** No matter what role we occupy, we almost always need others to succeed. Look across the spectrum of your life. Is there anything you do that doesn't depend on the contribution of at least one other person? The truth is that, in almost all situations, we can do better with the help of others rather than when we go it alone. Once we get this, we will dedicate ourselves to dealing with others in the spirit of Mutual Win.

3. **I must be curious.** Mutual Win requires two significant bits of information. The first is a clear, deep idea of what is a win for us. The

second is a clear, complete grasp of what is a win for the other person. To find the mutually beneficial solution to differences and disagreements, we must curiously seek to clearly know what is our own win as well as what is a win for the other.

Generosity

I suppose I am like most people in that I love the Christmas season. One of my favorite holiday indulgences is to watch the re-runs of the classic Christmas movies: *A Miracle on 34th Street, It's a Wonderful Life, A Christmas Story, National Lampoon's Christmas Vacation*, and Charles Dickens' *A Christmas Carol.*

A couple of Decembers ago, my wife and I took our son Gabriel to see a stage production of *A Christmas Carol.* Remember that Ebenezer Scrooge was a grasping miser who cared only about money, shutting out all human warmth, and treating people with no compassion or concern. To him, people were only tools to help him line his pockets.

The dramatic center of this fable occurred on Christmas Eve, when three ghosts who conducted what we would today call an intervention visited him while he slept. They forced him to take a critical look at his life and gave him an opportunity to transform his heart.

The Ghost of Christmas Past transported Scrooge back to his youth, where he saw the family warmth and happiness he no longer had. The Ghost of Christmas Present took him to the home of his employee Bob Cratchit, whose family bathed themselves in love for each other despite the impending death of their beloved son, Tiny Tim. The Ghost of Christmas Future took him forward to his forlorn gravesite with no one present to remember or care that he had lived or died.

Sure enough, the intervention worked. Scrooge faced up to the waste and barrenness that was his life. Awakening on Christmas Day to find himself still alive, he was a newborn man. He bounded out his front door, seeing every person he met as an opportunity to make their life nicer, warmer, and richer. Right before our eyes, he became a living, breathing source of generosity.

The spirit of generosity – what a gift to give others! Imagine adding this spirit to our mindset. Imagine the positive impact we'd have on others with a willingness to be relentlessly generous with them. Imagine the goodwill we'd create by being determined to leave no encounter without some small act of generosity. Imagine how attractive we'd become to most everyone we run across.

I want to emphasize that by generosity I do not mean giving tangible things to people, though doing so might indeed be an act of generosity. Think of it more as a gift of self. I think of a married couple I now counsel whose relationship was wrecked by conflict and ill will. Though they learned and used sound communication skills, it was when they each adopted a posture of generosity toward each other that their relationship began to soar. Without me giving any instructions as to exactly how to act, they became attentive to each other, went out of their way to express affection, and overlooked or forgave the slights they once escalated into atrocities.

Here, then, are three mindsets that can help you adopt a spirit of generosity in all your relationships, whether they be personal or professional, intimate or casual:

1. **I can make a difference.** We most likely do not have the power to transform the planet, but we can make a profound difference with people within our little corner of the world. Keep alive this belief and we will act to do so. Start with our immediate family, then focus on our friends and colleagues, and go from there to the chance encounters we have with people during our day. We can and will impact them by acting with this spirit of generosity.

2. **Think globally, act locally.** A conviction I hold is that, if each person in the world went home each evening and treated the members of their family generously, the world would be transformed. So, all we have to do is be aware of the opportunities that exist with the people in our life to find ways to express generosity. As with the couple mentioned previously, we do not need a skill-building course, just a healthy dose of an awareness of the opportunities and a willingness to act with generosity.

3. **What goes around comes around.** What we sow we reap. By acting toward people with the spirit of generosity, we will, without question, make a positive impression, even elicit affection, so that they will almost for sure be motivated to respond in kind. We now have an ally, someone to call upon when needed in our pursuit of the great results we want. Be aware of the benefits to us by our generosity to others.

Empathic Compassion

Being treated with compassion is perhaps the greatest yearning of the human heart. When treated with compassion, no one, except perhaps the most hardened psychopath, can resist feeling warm toward the giver and wanting to give back in return.

Empathic compassion is the ability to understand another person's inner experience and to respond accordingly. Typically, we train people to actively listen in order to demonstrate this. People are taught to look past the ideas a person expresses to their feelings and to send a message recognizing these feelings. "You sure are upset by his behavior, aren't you?" "I can see how truly excited you are about that good news." "What I hear you saying is that you are profoundly sad about your youngest child going off to college." These are examples of empathic, compassionate active listening.

When we make people feel heard and understood, not only at the idea level, but at the feeling level as well, we communicate that they are valued and worth our time and energy. They feel valued and in turn will value us enough to align with us.

To help us grow our empathic compassion quotient, adopt and remember the following mindsets:

1. **People hunger for compassion.** It bears repeating that the greatest yearning of the human heart is to be heard and understood. Compassion is perhaps the greatest gift one can give to another. It is as vital for emotional well-being as air is for physical survival. Once we truly appreciate this, we can then tune into people's heart and spirit needs, as well as into their body and mind ones.

2. **Opportunities abound.** As with Ebenezer Scrooge, every encounter we have with another person is an opportunity to act with empathic compassion. But, it's even more than that. In every encounter we have with another, we are going to either communicate "I care" or "I could care less." In other words, we cannot not communicate our compassion or lack thereof to each and every person we run across. Do you really want to miss the opportunity to deliver empathic compassion or, even worse, give off vibes of indifference or disdain?

3. **What goes around comes around.** Remember that people do not separate us from our role, our goals, or our message. If they feel positive about us, they are more likely to feel positive about what we say to them and what we want from them. They will thereby be more willing to go that extra mile for us. We, therefore, want to present to people the kind of person who will naturally attract them to us. We want to bathe them in such compassion that they will be willing to help us produce our great results.

THE INTERPERSONAL INTELLIGENCE WORKSHOP

At first blush, you might doubt that you can increase your Interpersonal Intelligence quotient. After all, you may think that the five components require sainthood of you.

I urge you to rid yourself of this self-limiting view. After all, habits of mind can be learned and grown. You need not reach perfection; all you need to do is to increase your Interpersonal Intelligence quotient to a level at which you will make yourself more attractive to others so that they will want to help you succeed.

What follows is the four-step Interpersonal Intelligence workshop. With or without the guidance and support of your therapist, consultant, or coach, I predict that you will quickly see the results, both in terms of how people respond to you and in your personal satisfaction, if you avidly tackle it.

Step One: Develop Self-Awareness

Step One will help you assess how developed you are with regard to the five Interpersonal Intelligence traits. You are to rate yourself from 1 to 10 (with 1 being lowest and 10 highest) in each of the five traits and then note what you could do to rate higher on each. Please refer back to the discussion of these traits if needed.

1. **Kindness**

$1 - 2 - 3 - 4 - 5 - 6 - 7 - 8 - 9 - 10$

_____

_____

_____

2. **Appreciation**

$1 - 2 - 3 - 4 - 5 - 6 - 7 - 8 - 9 - 10$

_____

_____

_____

3. **Mutual Win**

$1 - 2 - 3 - 4 - 5 - 6 - 7 - 8 - 9 - 10$

_____

_____

_____

4. **Generosity**

$1 - 2 - 3 - 4 - 5 - 6 - 7 - 8 - 9 - 10$

_____

_____

_____

5. **Empathic Compassion**

$1 - 2 - 3 - 4 - 5 - 6 - 7 - 8 - 9 - 10$

_____

_____

_____

Step Two: Plan Your Action

My assumption is that you scored high on at least one or two of these Interpersonal Intelligence traits. For these, record below those situations in your life in which it is important for you to continue to act out these traits. Who are the key people in each of these situations? Exactly what will you do with these people in this situation to continue to act mindfully with regard to this trait? The key word is "mindfully"; the more you act with mindfulness, the more ingrained both the underlying mindsets and their resulting behaviors become.

Interpersonal Intelligence Trait: _____

	Situation	People	What
1.	_____	_____	_____
	_____	_____	_____
2.	_____	_____	_____
	_____	_____	_____
3.	_____	_____	_____
	_____	_____	_____

Interpersonal Intelligence Trait: _____

	Situation	People	What
1.	_____	_____	_____
	_____	_____	_____
2.	_____	_____	_____
	_____	_____	_____
3.	_____	_____	_____
	_____	_____	_____

I also assume that you, dear reader, being human, did not score high in at least one, two, or perhaps even three of the Interpersonal Intelligence traits. If I am correct, this is an opportunity for you to grow these. Note below those traits in which you are weak. For each, note the situations in your life that present opportunities to use these traits, who are the key people in these situations, and what you could do to act better according to these traits.

Interpersonal Intelligence Trait: _____

	Situation	People	What
1.			
2.			
3.			

Interpersonal Intelligence Trait: _____

	Situation	People	What
1.			
2.			
3.			

Interpersonal Intelligence Trait: _____

	Situation	People	What
1.			
2.			
3.			

Step Three: Determine Your Mindset

You will remember that each of the Interpersonal Intelligence traits depends on three mindsets. With these mindsets in place, you will find it easy to act out these traits. Without these mindsets, it will be next to impossible for you to deliver on them.

Note below the three most important mindsets you need to ingrain in order to consistently act with Interpersonal Intelligence.

Mindset 1: _____

_____

Mindset 2: _____

_____

Mindset 3: _____

_____

You don't want to leave to chance your ability to keep these mindsets at the forefront of your consciousness. You want to rehearse and practice them so that when a moment of truth arrives you are likely to have them in mind. Some people select an early morning time to set their mental tone for the day. Others will preview the upcoming day and rehearse the mindsets they need in the various critical situations. Still others use 3 × 5 inch cards containing their key mindsets to refer to periodically as the day progresses. Your task here is to devise your daily mindset development plan.

My Mindset Development Plan: _____

_____

_____

_____

_____

_____

Step Four: Gather Your Support

It is difficult to adopt anything new without a support person. This person can be invaluable in providing feedback, patting you on the back when you get discouraged, giving you salient advice, and cheerleading your successes. Write below whom you will enlist to be your support person and exactly what you will ask this person to do to support you as you grow your Interpersonal Intelligence.

My support person: _____

What I will ask this person to do: _____

_____

_____

_____

INTENSIFIERS

Congratulations on your good work on the Interpersonal Intelligence workshop. If you follow through on your plan for the next month or so, you will almost certainly reap the results. Here now are three intensifiers that can further help you deepen and make vibrant your ability to act with Interpersonal Intelligence.

Cultivate Gratitude

In Chapter 6, I emphasize the importance of focus. If a person chooses to focus on what is wrong in life, who is to blame for misfortunes, and why things might not turn out the way wanted, this person will sour his or her mind and sap his or her energy. Not inconsequentially, this person certainly will not come across as very attractive to others.

To the contrary, focusing on what is good and positive in life – holding an attitude of gratitude – will warm a person on the inside and bathe others in his or her glow. Here are five strategies you can use to cultivate your gratitude quotient:

1. Start off each day by purposely focusing on what you have in your life about which you can be grateful. By consciously identifying these in the morning, you can set a positive, even joyful tone for the day.
2. Before bedtime, note the good things that happened that day. A participant in one of my seminars put a marble in a glass container each night for each good thing that she experienced that day. When the container became full, she treated herself to some celebratory reward (e.g., dinner and a movie), then emptied the jar to start over the next day. This will make you smile from the inside out.
3. Stop complaining. We become so accustomed to complaining about life's little setbacks that we often don't even realize we're doing it. Not only to be happy, but also to be attractive to others, stop doing that.

4. Develop your savoring buds. Coping has to do with solving one's problems and setbacks, while savoring means reveling in what's good. When you experience something positive, take time to pay attention to it. Think about the taste of the ice cream in your mouth; linger over the pleasure of hugging those special people in your life; soak up the warmth of your hot bath. Above all, take a mental photograph of your good experiences and be sure to celebrate them with your significant others.

5. Show gratitude to others. John F. Kennedy once said, "As we express our gratitude, we must never forget that the highest appreciation is not to utter words, but to live by them" (Kennedy, 1963). Thank people. Tell loved ones what they have meant to you. Let people know how happy you are to be so blessed in your life.

These five strategies can form a template for your life. They will not only warm your heart, but also the hearts of others. They will intensify your Interpersonal Intelligence.

Get Feedback

One of the more innovative secrets to marital success is to ask your spouse this question: What's it like to be married to me? If you are open to and take seriously the answer you get, you have an opportunity to adjust your behavior in order to be most satisfying to your partner. Your marriage can then soar. Feedback is not only critical for marital success, but for virtually everything in life as well: customer service, athletic performance, parenting, and teaching, to name just a few.

Since Interpersonal Intelligence starts with non-tangible inner qualities, it is difficult to translate them into observable behavior. It is therefore difficult to get a clear sense of the degree to which you operate in an intelligent interpersonal manner. It behooves you, then, to get feedback on your Interpersonal Intelligence performance. With someone you trust to be honest with you, regularly ask: How am I doing with regard to treating people with kindness? Showing appreciation? Conducting my relations from the Mutual Win principle? Acting from a spirit of generosity? Displaying empathic compassion? You can refine these questions with specifics: With whom? Where? When?

The answers you get to these questions can be very valuable to you. They tell you what, where, and when you do well. Perhaps more importantly, they alert you to what you need to stop doing, what you need to alter, and what you need to start doing. By implementing what you learn, you then raise your Interpersonal Intelligence quotient, the end result being people willing to commit to helping you create your great results.

Develop Perspective

One of the common mistakes people make to drive themselves to distraction is to blow relatively minor things out of proportion. When encountering annoyances or hassles, some people habitually catastrophize. Thinking their hardships to be awful, horrible, or terrible, they regularly create worry, stress, and anxiety for themselves. They thereby block their ability to act in an interpersonally intelligent manner, instead coming across as distracted, self-absorbed, and irritable, qualities hardly designed to be attractive to others.

While there are certainly things that are severe enough to warrant serious upset (we would agree, for instance, that the death of one's child would be one), virtually nothing negative that we encounter rises to the level of awful, horrible, or terrible. On a scale of badness from 1 to 100, where the death of a child would rate somewhere between 95 and 100, most all the hardships we face fall within the 1–20 range. Wouldn't these qualify as dislikable, frustrating, or crummy, but not catastrophic?

Basketball coach Mike Krzyzewski reports that Duke University president Richard Broadhead once said to him, "You outlive your darkest day" (Krzyzewski, 2000, p. 4). Indeed, keeping things in perspective helps us keep a sunny disposition. I think it wise to follow the prescription of Dr. Richard Carlson, "Don't sweat the small stuff . . . and it's all small stuff" (Carlson, 1997).

AN ORGANIZATIONAL CASE STUDY

It was abundantly clear that a lack of Interpersonal Intelligence was the culprit when I spoke by phone to Mark, the general manager of a large Midwestern bank. It turned out that he had received rather scathing reviews from his direct reports on his 360° Feedback Survey for the previous 12-month period. "I've got to do something or I'll lose them all," he said, a tone of desperation in his voice.

A detailed discussion showed Mark to be a harsh taskmaster. He appropriately expected extraordinary performance from his people, but reported that he rarely complimented, praised, or rewarded them. When I asked him to estimate what percentage of his interactions with his leadership team were positive, negative, and neutral, he said 10%, 45%, and 45%.

Following this, we had a long conversation about the value of trust in any relationship, be it business, friendship, or family. I pulled no punches when I told him that his leadership style was not only a sure-fire trustbuster, but also a spawning ground for resentment and anger – hardly the type of feelings that would motivate his people to act relentlessly to produce great results.

We then arranged a series of twice-per-month phone appointments devoted to raising his kindness and appreciation quotient. I first addressed his expectations for error-free performance from his management team and his habit of attacking not only their performance but their character as well. I showed him how unrealistic these expectations were and how counterproductive his personal attacks were. I then instructed him to daily do the very same process I outlined in Chapter 4's Fearlessness workshop: (1) recognize his anger moments; (2) track down his perfectionistic self-talk (e.g., "He should have thought of that before he acted"); (3) actively dispute his perfectionistic thinking so as to see how unrealistic and counterproductive it is; (4) reformulate his anger-producing thinking; and (5) act with kindness and appreciation.

By doing this exercise each day for the better part of a month, he reported that he was beginning to catch his perfectionistic thinking on the fly and correct his negative thinking immediately in his head. He started to accept the intrinsic fallibility of people and to let go of his judgmental way of thinking about them. Coincidently, he found himself experiencing less exasperation and reacting with anger less reflexively.

Co-existent with this, I coached Mark to express acts of appreciation to his people. With the assumption that practice builds habits, he began to purposely look for positive behaviors to praise, deliver "thank yous," and express appreciation when he saw them do something correct.

As two months turned into three, it became clear to me that Mark was transforming himself from being limited to being competent with regard to his Interpersonal Intelligence. He felt better, his people felt better, and management teamwork began humming.

To sum, then, consider the following organizational principles:

- Those in leadership roles must be exemplary models of Interpersonal Intelligence. If those at the top do not live it, no one else will.
- Interpersonal Intelligence must be a major component of hiring, employee evaluation, promotion, and termination. In other words, it should be incorporated into the fabric of the organization's culture.
- Because there is nowhere in our education system where the five traits of Interpersonal Intelligence are taught, training in Interpersonal Intelligence must be incorporated into a company's training program. This training must be experiential, deep, and on-going.
- A major function of leadership is to facilitate employee growth. On-going coaching in both job competency and Interpersonal Intelligence must be a key leadership responsibility. Opportunities for coaching are boundless such that those in leadership roles – executives, managers, and supervisors – need to regularly take advantage of these opportunities.
- Teamwork should be emphasized. A company need not adopt a team-based culture to expect individuals, groups, and departments to team up. However, cooperation, communication, and teamwork must be the by-word.

A FINAL WORD

We truly live in an interdependent world in which we can almost always accomplish more with the help and cooperation of others than by ourselves. Those who develop the traits that comprise Interpersonal Intelligence gain a tremendous advantage in life. They not only experience the pleasures and joys these traits bring them, but they also gain the allegiance from others needed to create their great results.

I urge you to actively and energetically use the Interpersonal Intelligence workshop to grow the traits of kindness, appreciation, Mutual Win, generosity, and empathic compassion. You will see the extraordinary benefits to both your emotional well-being and to your productivity.

REFERENCES AND SUGGESTED READING

Beatles, The (2000). *The Beatles anthology*. San Francisco, CA: Chronicle Books, LLC.
Bennett, W. J. (1993). *The book of virtues*. New York: Simon & Schuster.
Carlson, R. (1997). *Don't sweat the small stuff and it's all small stuff*. New York: Hyperion.
Covey, S. R. (1989). *The 7 habits of highly effective people*. New York: Simon & Schuster.
Gibbs, J. (2002). *Racing to win*. Colorado Springs, CO: Moltnomah Books.
Goldman, D. (1995). *Emotional intelligence*. New York: Bantam Books.
Kennedy, J. F. (1963). "Proclamation 3560 – Thanksgiving Day, 1963." Available at: www.presidency.ucsb.edu/ws/?pid=9511 (accessed November 16, 2016).
Krzyzewski, M. (2000). *Leading with the heart*. New York: Warner Books, Inc.
McCullough, D. (2006). *1776*. New York: Simon & Schuster.
Peterson, C., & Seligman, M. E. P. (2004). *Character strengths and virtues*. New York: Oxford University Press.
Rubenstein, E. (n.d.). "Start with the heart." *Edutopia*. Available at: www.edutopia.org/louisville-sel-social-emotional-learning (accessed November 16, 2016).
Ryan, M. J. (1999). *Attitudes of gratitude*. New York: MJF Books.
Supreme Court Justice's characterization of pornography rendered in comments re Jacobellis vs. Ohio (No. 11) 6/22/64.

CHAPTER 6

Mental Muscle

The tools to build mental toughness –
the Power of Focus and the Power of Belief

Our most intimate relationship is the one we have with our minds.
Byron Katie

To get orientated with Mental Muscle, take a few minutes to think of someone you believe to be mentally strong. What are the characteristics that give this person such grit? What are the defining qualities that spawn this person's strength?

Chances are that you've described this person along the following lines. He or she is clear about and stays focused on his or her goals, even in the face of adversity.

This person has a "can-and-will-do" attitude. There is a focus on problem solving when facing obstacles, not whining, self-pitying, or finger pointing. There is a certain grace about this person through thick and thin.

I bet that most if not all of these descriptions typify the person you identified. The person I think of is Jerry Sloan, the former Utah Jazz basketball coach and member of the Naismith Basketball Hall of Fame. Jerry and I were teammates on two NCAA Championship-winning teams at the University of Evansville before he launched his professional career, first as a player and then as a coach.

I have never known anyone more tough-minded than Jerry. He was totally focused. He was relentless. Whether in games or in practice, he put out 100% effort every second he was on the court. He never backed down nor ever gave up, fighting tooth and nail till the final buzzer. It made no difference if we were ahead or behind, Jerry played as if possessed by the Tasmanian devil.

Although Jerry might not appreciate me sharing this, I remember an incident during our senior year, far from the public eye. Already a two-time All-American first teamer, it seems that he had broken some minor team rule. Arriving at the gym the next day, I found Jerry doggedly running laps around our double workout court for the whole hour before practice.

I have long forgotten the rule Jerry broke, but I have not forgotten the intensity with which he ran his laps, nor how hard he pushed himself through the two-hour scrimmage that followed. His jaw was set, his eyes were intense, and there was a no-nonsense message in his face and body. It was as if he were communicating, "Nobody, not even you, Coach, is going to break me; I will never give in to fatigue or fear; I will not let you or anyone defeat me."

Notice in my example, as well as in yours, that we are not talking about physical, but mental strength: Mental Muscle. Jerry was the most mentally tough person I have ever known. Sure he was gifted with exquisite athletic ability and a deep knowledge of the game. But I have no doubt that his mental strength contributed greatly to the success he had in the highly competitive world of professional basketball. The person you selected most assuredly is as tough of mind as him.

So, a hallmark of people who produce great results is Mental Muscle. Whether we talk about Mahatma Gandhi, Nelson Mandela, Winston Churchill, Michael Jordan, or Ronald Reagan, they possessed toughness in two mental muscles: the Power of Focus and the Power of Belief.

THE POWER OF FOCUS

The Power of Focus rests on the fact that what we focus on largely determines how we react. Imagine if for a few weeks you focused exclusively on the hardships and hassles in your life. You would find that your mood would almost certainly descend into doom, gloom, and defeat. To the contrary, focusing exclusively on those bright and shiny things in your life would raise your spirits and kindle your well-being.

Our focus not only helps determine our mood, but it also impacts how we act. This explains the drive we bring to producing results when we focus on our goals, our vision for the future, and our life's Passionate Purpose. By focusing on these as yet unattained results, we are propelled to act to make them a reality. What better example of this is there than President John F. Kennedy's 1962 commitment to land a man on the moon and return him safely to earth before the end of the 1960s. Focusing on this goal drove thousands of NASA employees to do what was necessary to make it happen.

My task now is to show you how to develop the Power of Focus, thereby igniting your Unrelenting Drive, Dedication, and Determination. You can do so through mastering two skills: (1) leveraging pleasure and pain; and (2) harnessing rewards and punishments.

Focus Factor 1: Leveraging Pleasure and Pain

As with all other species, we humans are wired to seek pleasure and to avoid pain. This pleasure–pain principle is a fundamental law of human nature. It pervades almost all our actions, affects virtually all our decisions, and even explains many of the ridiculous, self-defeating choices we make. All things being equal, we act to experience immediate pleasure and to not experience immediate pain, even when to do so may cause us harm in the long run.

To see how powerful the pleasure–pain principle is, take a look through the fabric of your life. Think about the anticipated pleasure that drives you to devour that bowl of ice cream that you know will pack inches around your waist. How about the pain you avoid when you put off preparing your income tax returns until the last possible minute? Remember how hard you work for the pleasure of that smile, pat on the back, or compliment from your spouse, cherished friend, or colleague.

So, pleasure and pain drives us. But there's the rub. We humans often let pleasure and pain run us, rather than purposely using pleasure and pain to our advantage. In the service of avoiding pain, we often mindlessly default to procrastinating from doing all kinds of constructive things, such as balancing the checkbook, cleaning the house, and getting the annual medical check-up. In order to secure immediate pleasure, we often mindlessly engage in all sorts of foolish activities, such as eating that extra helping of pasta, buying that dress we can't really afford, or drinking that extra cocktail. An with Bob, below, we often allow pleasure and pain to run us to our detriment.

The Case of Bob

Twenty-four-year-old Bob sought me out to help him overcome his cocaine addiction. With desperation in his voice, he confessed that he had failed to beat this drug habit through two 30-day in-patient programs and three out-patient psychotherapists.

I must admit that I wondered if I could help him when numerous other competent clinicians had already failed. I knew that I had to come up with something to break through whatever the barriers were to his recovery. With fingers crossed, I instructed him to compile as comprehensive and profound a list as he could of all the benefits (pleasures) and costs (pain) to both doing and not doing cocaine.

Bob appeared at his next appointment with such a list, illustrated in Figure 6.1. Then came the critical moment. With as much gravity as I could muster, I first asked him whether, when he contemplated doing cocaine, he focused on the pleasures or the pains. Without hesitation, he said, "The pleasures." Reversing the question, I then asked him whether he focused on the pleasures or the pains when he thought about not doing cocaine. He emphatically stated, "The pains."

There it was. Note how pleasure and pain had heretofore provided a powerful, insurmountable barrier to this young man's ability to defeat his cocaine addiction. He exclusively focused on the pleasures of doing cocaine and the pains of not doing cocaine. No wonder he failed in his five prior therapeutic attempts to break this nasty addiction: with this focus, his only incentive was to do cocaine. He

Doing Cocaine

Benefits/Pleasures

- The unbelievable feel-good
- Women seek me out
- The thrill of the score
- Dulls my pain
- Part of my social network

Costs/Pains

- Will never amount to anything
- Parents will disown me
- No decent woman would have me
- Lose my self-respect
- Missed opportunities for closeness

Not Doing Cocaine

Benefits/Pleasures

- Potential for a great life
- Save tons of money
- Keep the love/loyalty of my family
- Never have to hide or pretend
- Never have to look over my shoulder

Costs/Pains

- Face life without a crutch
- Loss of some friends
- Loss of the cocaine high
- Loss of the thrill of the score
- No escape hatch

FIGURE 6.1   Bob's Pleasure/Pain Analysis

clearly needed to reverse his pleasure–pain focus by connecting pain to doing cocaine and pleasure to not doing it.

After explaining all this to Bob, he and I then worked on strategies he could use to leverage pleasure and pain to his advantage. We came up with two ideas that were very practical, both involving writing on one side of a 4 × 6 inch card the profound pains of doing cocaine and on the other the substantial pleasures of not doing cocaine. One strategy was to reflect six times a day (breakfast, mid-morning, lunch, mid-afternoon, supper, mid-evening) on the respective pleasures and pains. A second was to pull out this card and remind himself of the benefits of choosing to not do cocaine and the costs of doing cocaine any time he felt even the slightest temptation to indulge himself.

I am happy to report that Bob's leveraging of pleasure and pain to his advantage gave him the Mental Muscle to fully use his subsequent therapy to kick his cocaine habit. As I write this, he has been free of cocaine for five years.

As with Bob, all of us would be wise to purposely leverage pleasure and pain to meet our great goals. It will work for us as it did for Bob in producing the great results we want.

Focus Factor 2: Harnessing Rewards and Punishments

Rewards and punishments are used daily to influence people to act in desired ways. Parents routinely ply their kids with such perks as money, videogames, and special privileges to encourage good grades. Airlines award frequent flyer miles to entice people to choose to travel on their planes. Saloons sponsor two-for-the-price-of-one drink nights to lure customers to their establishment.

Conversely, law enforcement officers attempt to discourage speeding by punishing offending motorists with traffic tickets. The state inflicts the death penalty in part to discourage people from committing heinous crimes. Parents ground their children in an attempt to reduce or eliminate offensive behavior.

Rewards and punishments capitalize on a fundamental law of learning discovered by the famous behavioral psychologist B. F. Skinner (1974). This states that what follows a behavior has a powerful effect on future behavior. Rewarding a behavior encourages that behavior in the future, while punishing a behavior has the effect of decreasing that behavior going forward. We can harness this law to our own advantage if we so choose.

The Case of Jonas

Purposely utilizing the power of rewards and punishments proved instrumental in helping Jonas, a 48-year-old novelist caught in the grip of a severe episode of procrastination he called writer's block. To the frustration of his publisher, the chagrin of his wife, and the disgust of himself, he found it next to impossible to knuckle down to work on his latest opus.

Despite my best efforts, none of the insights I provided nor the strategies I offered helped Jonas to break through his procrastination. Finally, out of desperation, I harnessed the power of rewards and punishments. Witness the following conversation he and I had:

Dr. G.:   Jonas, we've tried many techniques to help you knuckle down and apply yourself to your work. I think it's time to get tough with you.

Jonas: What do you mean?

Dr. G.:   Let's use rewards and punishments. First, what is something you find pleasurable that is available to you every day?

Jonas: I enjoy reading the newspapers and the various books next to my bed.

Dr. G.:   OK. Let's make a rule. We'll use reading as a reward. The rule will be that you're only permitted to read the newspaper or any other enjoyable material if you first put in two hours of work on your novel. If you don't do your work, no reading. Period. Will you agree to that?

Jonas: Sure.

Dr. G.:   Great. Now think about something painful or onerous that is available to you every day.

Jonas:	I hate Hillary Clinton. I can't stand to even see her face on TV.
Dr. G.:	So, you're on the conservative side of the political spectrum, are you?
Jonas:	Yep. She drives me to distraction. God forbid she should ever become president.
Dr. G.:	OK. I'll tell you what. You bring to me ten crisp $100 bills. Each day that you don't do your two hours of writing, I'll send one of your $100 bills to her presidential campaign committee. How about that?
Jonas:	That's horrible. I could never bring myself to do that.
Dr. G.:	But, that's the point, isn't it? You never have to send her one penny. By focusing on the punishment of sending her the money, as well as the pleasure of getting to do your reading, you can be driven to honor your writing commitment. To decide to procrastinate is the decision to support her political ambitions, plus to not having your reading pleasures that day.
Jonas:	OK, I'll do it.

Harnessing the power of rewards and punishments worked wonders for Jonas. The punishing threat of helping send Hillary Clinton to the White House motivated Jonas to get to work. Though he slipped up once in the first week of his reward–punishment program, he became so focused on avoiding this onerous consequence that writing his novel became a pleasure. He clearly realized that choosing to goof off at home would help to put his liberal adversary on the track to the presidency. The combination of losing his reward and suffering his dreaded punishment heightened his focus on making the best decision each day in order to meet his long-term goal of getting his next novel onto the bookshelves.

As with Jonas, harnessing rewards and punishments can help all of us become so mentally focused we most surely will make the right choices vis-à-vis acting to realize our great goals. Moreover, over time we will strengthen our mental toughness, thereby finding it easy to display the Unrelenting Drive, Dedication, and Determination we need to produce our extraordinary results.

THE POWER OF FOCUS WORKSHOP

The Power of Focus workshop is straightforward. You clinicians, consultants, and coaches can work your clients through this five-step process in your office or simply assign it to be completed before your next meeting. Regardless of the process you choose, take pains to follow up by making sure your client did it correctly.

And you, dear layperson, please commit to doing an exceptional job on completing this workshop. More importantly, follow through on it with action. The more you use it, the more habitual it will become, gradually honing your

Mental Muscle, and strengthening your Unrelenting Drive, Dedication, and Determination.

Step One: State Your Goal

As a first step, clearly state the result you want to produce. Bob would have stated, "My goal is to stop using cocaine," and Jonas would have said, "I will work two hours daily on my novel." State it in positive terms, as per "I will do X," and make it concise and precise.

_____

_____

_____

Step Two: Leverage Pleasure and Pain

The second step is to leverage pleasure and pain. Similar to what Bob did, list all the pleasures or benefits you will get from achieving your goal. Pay special attention to the more profound pleasures, being sure to consider both the long-term ones as well as the more immediate ones. Similarly, list all the profound costs or pains you will experience if you do not produce these results. Be expansive. Then, like Bob, create a plan to keep yourself focused on these pleasures and pains.

Profound pleasures or benefits from producing my desired results: _____

_____

_____

_____

Profound pains or costs from failing to produce my results: _____

_____

_____

_____

My plan to keep focused on the pleasures and pains: _____

_____

_____

_____

Step Three: Harness Rewards and Punishments

The third step is to select the exact rewards and punishments you will use to help keep you focused on acting to produce your great results. Refer to Jonas as an example if you wish. Just make sure that your rewards are sufficiently pleasurable to stimulate you to act and that your punishments are sufficiently onerous to discourage you from not acting.

Rewards for acting: _____

_____

_____

_____

Punishments for not acting: _____

_____

_____

_____

Step Four: Gather Your Support

It is difficult to adopt new patterns by oneself. A support system helps. Here you are to identify someone you trust to help you with your Power of Focus program. Name this person and determine exactly what you will ask him or her to do to help you.

My support person: _____

What I will ask this person to do: _____

_____

_____

_____

Step Five: Review and Revise Action Plan

Never leave an action-planning session without a strategy for review and revision. Determine when and where you will assess the success or failure of your Power of Focus action plan.

Where and when I will critically review my plan: _____

_____

_____

_____

Congratulations. You have started the process of applying the Power of Focus to developing the Mental Muscle needed to produce the great results you want. The more skillful you become in this, and the more ingrained you make it, the easier and easier you will find it to sustain the action necessary to realize the results you want.

THE POWER OF BELIEF

As explained in Chapter 1, we have discovered something quite remarkable about human nature in the last 30 years or so, something that is as substantial in human terms as gravity is to the physical universe. Quite simply, it is that the way we process what we encounter in our brains – through our beliefs, our paradigms, and our habits of thinking – determines in large measure how we react.

It makes no difference whether our beliefs are sensible, rational, or an accurate representation of reality; we respond consistent with what we believe to be true. If you believe it correct to stop your car at a red light, you will do so. If, as a terrorist, you believe killing Westerners is your sacred duty, you will. If you believe yourself to be a kangaroo, you will hop around rather than walk. Our beliefs drive our emotions, our actions, and even our physiology. This is the power of our beliefs.

This is not psychobabble. Through thousands of research studies and millions of case examples, we know to be true what the ancient Greek philosopher Epictetus told us over 2,000 years ago: "Men are not disturbed by things, but by the view which they take of them" (Epictetus, 1948, p. 19). This discovery has revolutionized the treatment of such psychological conditions as depression, anxiety, and substance abuse, and it has transformed the field of human drive, dedication, and determination.

As taught by the great American psychologist Dr. Albert Ellis (1997), the Power of Belief can be captured in a straightforward ABC model (see Figure 4.1). In this model, A stands for the Activating Event, or the situation with which we are contending; B represents our Belief about the A; and C stands for the Consequence, or the way we react behaviorally, emotionally, and physiologically. The key: it is the B, our belief, that causes the C, our reaction, not the A, the thing we encounter.

Activating Event	Belief	Behavioral/Emotional Consequence

Activates   Causes

A ═══════════════════⟹ B ═══════════════════⟹ C

Personal Responsibility
Empowerment
Choice

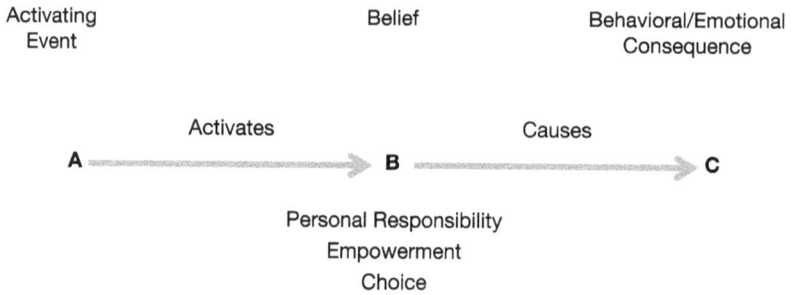

FIGURE 6.2   The Power of Belief

Imagine, for example, that you are to give an important sales presentation. This is the Activating Event (the A). Think how different you would react at C if you strongly believed, at B, "I can do this – they'll love what I have to say," rather than, "I'll never pull this off – they'll think I'm a dunce." The A is the same, but with the first B you would experience calmness and self-confidence, and would be raring to go; with the second B, you would feel anxiety and dread, and would be pushed to run away and hide.

So, this ABC model not only communicates a scientific reality, but it can also greatly empower us, for it is a model of personal responsibility. It tells us that we author how we react across situations; in other words, we are not compelled to react in a particular way to circumstances, but we react by virtue of "our view of them." Realizing that we own our beliefs (since they are in our mind), we are empowered to take charge of our reactions by working to adopt beliefs that stimulate us to act productively. The bottom line is that we can choose what we believe and thereby how we act. What potential strength we have!

People with Mental Muscle, like my teammate Jerry Sloan, have mastered not only the Power of Focus, but the Power of Belief as well. Specifically, they have mastered two cornerstones of belief technology: (1) they've rid themselves of drive-killing beliefs; and (2) they've made an art of operating on empowering, self-enhancing ones.

Belief Factor 1: Eradicating Drive-Killing Beliefs

Drive-killing beliefs inhibit us from relentlessly acting to produce our great results. They prompt us to act in ways that move us in the opposite direction. To have Mental Muscle, we must destroy our Killer Bs.

The Five Killer Bs

Drive-killing beliefs come in five categories:

1. **Low frustration tolerance** (LFT). LFT beliefs cause a person to over-react emotionally to hardships, setbacks, and hassles. Even worse, they prompt us to avoid difficult challenges, to procrastinate, and to give up before reaching desired results. People who hold LFT beliefs tend to think along the following lines:

    *   "This is *too hard*."
    *   "It's *horrible* to have to face this hardship, put up with this hassle, and/or delay my immediate pleasure."
    *   "I *can't stand* doing this onerous chore and/or delaying my gratification."
    *   "It's *easier* to put it off and do it later" (when, of course, it will magically become easy and pleasurable).

    Note how self-defeating these beliefs are. They prompt a person to give up in the face of adversity, avoid the hard work necessary for success, and cut corners. They need to be replaced with more realistic habits of thinking that enable a person to tolerate frustration and persist when the going gets tough – to wit:

    *   "This may be hard, but it's *not too hard*."
    *   "It's certainly a hassle, but in no way is it *horrible*."
    *   "I may not enjoy doing the chore, but I *can easily stand it*."
    *   "It's ridiculous to think it's easier to put this chore off. If I don't knock it out now, I'll still have to do it later. *It's really easier to do it now*."

2. **Negativity.** The essence of the glass half empty, people mired in negativity focus on predicting the worst about the future. Thinking such things as, "It'll *never* work," "Nothing will ever change," or "They'll *never* buy this," these people often feel discouraged, hopeless, and powerless, even before they ever take action. They then find it next to impossible to summon the will to initiate and sustain the effort to produce great results.

    The antidote to negativity is not Pollyanna thinking, but what I call "realistic positivity." That is, while not denying the difficulties they face or the fact that indeed things may not turn out as they wish, people with realistic positivity eliminate habitual assumptions about the hopelessness of the future. They hold the beliefs: "I don't have a crystal ball, so I don't know if my efforts will produce results or not, but if it's going to be, it's up to me;" "You never know until you try;" or "Let's give it a shot and see what happens."

3. **Self-doubt.** Going for the gold requires boldness, some semblance of a devil-may-care attitude, and even courage. Who would be willing to lay it out there, take risks, and have a ball when mired in such self-doubting belief patterns as *"I can't do this," "It's too big for me,"* or *"I just don't have what it takes"*? The answer is: no one!

As Richard Bach said, "Argue for your limitations, and sure enough they're yours" (Bach, 1989, p. 75). Self-doubt cripples drive. It obliterates the sustained, relentless effort needed to produce great results. Clearly, self-doubting beliefs need to be replaced with self-confident ones. As with realistic positivity, self-confidence is not a grandiose belief in one's superstardom. Rather, it has to do with a realistic appreciation of one's intelligence, ability, and experience; when one finds oneself in virgin territory, one believes in one's ingenuity, ability to problem solve, and grit. Self-confidence then provides the springboard for action, action, action.

4. **Perfectionism.** Perfectionism is the poster child of all-or-none thinking. When locked into this Killer B, a person demands from himself or herself the very best, not every once in a while, but each and every time. By escalating a sensible desire for excellence, as in "I want to do this well," into a demand for perfection, as per "I must (have to, have got to, need to) do this perfectly well," one makes total, complete success a necessity. Perfection is the only acceptable possibility. Anything else is a failure.

Here are some variations on this perfectionistic theme:

- "I've *got to* succeed at this."
- "I *must do* well or else."
- "I *need to* impress these people."
- "I *must* win this."
- "I *need* their approval."

Believing that one absolutely must do well and be approved escalates doing well to a life-or-death level. This is the exact formula for creating the fear of failure that leads to avoidance or playing it safe. Perfectionism beliefs need to be replaced with beliefs that capture the best of two worlds: that is, for greatness, one needs to deeply want or desire to achieve one's goals, thereby motivating oneself to put out one's best effort; but, one also needs to be concurrently realistic, humbly recognizing that perfection is unattainable, that there is no law of nature demanding perfection, and that there is no catastrophe in a performance less than perfect. This perspective creates a mental space for an all-out effort without fear or apprehension.

5. **Resentment.** I don't know about you, but resentment compromises my willingness to put out. When facing a task with such Killer Bs as "*I shouldn't* have to do this," "This is *stupid / ridiculous / unfair*," or the world-famous, "*Screw it and screw you*," I tend to emotionally shut down and check out.

It is axiomatic that loving what we do (see Chapter 3) aids and abets Unrelenting Drive, Dedication, and Determination. Given, though, that it is impossible to always love every single aspect of what we do, we would be wise to eliminate all vestiges of resentment. This requires that we give up demanding perfection, meaning we accept that, realistically, at least at times, people and situations will present us with hardships, hassles, and thankless chores. This is life. We do not have to like it, but, to live and work without the debilitating effects of resentment, we need to come to grips with this fundamental truth.

The Good Riddance Toolbox

There are three insights required to eradicate our self-limiting beliefs. First, represented by the ABC model, it is that our beliefs contribute largely to how we run our lives. Second, it matters little where our self-limiting beliefs originated; they are in our heads and we would be wise to get rid of them. A third insight is that eradicating self-limiting beliefs takes hard, hard work, requiring repetition and effort.

To eradicate self-limiting beliefs, we can use two powerful weapons. They are our powerful allies in building Mental Muscle. The first is keen awareness, and the second is healthy skepticism.

1. **Keen awareness.** I don't know where or how he caught the bug, but my son Gabriel loves to fish. I watch with amazement at the time he spends preparing his pole, assembling his bait, and casting his line, time after time, sometimes for an hour or more, attempting to land a fish. He seems to enjoy the process as much or more than the catch.

    Watching him one day at the pond close to our house, I made note of the intrinsic unfairness embedded in the sport of fishing. The playing field is anything but level. Even if we factor out all the obvious advantages Gabriel has over the fish (most notably his intelligence and size), perhaps one advantage stands out above all others: his awareness. Gabriel knows the rules of the game from the get-go; with total awareness, he knows what he is after, he plots his strategy, and he consciously executes his attack. The fish does not know the game is on until once hooked; in a state of total ignorance, all the fish is after is its supper.

    The point is, of course, that awareness is a powerful ally. So many of us so much of the time process our self-limiting Killer Bs without the slightest awareness that they are in our heads and running our lives. We have so deeply endorsed them as God's gospel truth that we simply accept them as reality. They are habitual, automatic, and marginally conscious at best. Like Gabriel does to the fish, they hook us, outside our awareness. It is a tremendous advantage to be conscious of our Killer Bs, for then we can systematically and cold-bloodedly destroy them.

2. **Healthy skepticism.** None of our beliefs are true just because we believe them. They are only true if, in fact, there is evidence and logic to support them. Our negative, Killer Bs are exactly that: beliefs, not necessarily facts. The world was never flat, although almost everyone once believed it to be. You are not incapable, the task at hand need not be done perfectly, and the chore is not too hard just because you think so.

Given this, we have not only the right, but the responsibility to be skeptical of our own beliefs. That is, we would be wise to hold our beliefs as hypotheses to be tested, not as facts to be automatically swallowed as true. One of the best questions ever invented is: Is this belief true or valid? This question gives us power. It gives us the ability to discern which of our beliefs have validity, the ability to alter our self-limiting beliefs if proven invalid, and then the freedom to act to create that greatness we value with better, self-empowering ones.

In *The Iliad*, Homer wrote, "We, the gods, will live so long as the humans believe in us. The day the humans no longer believe in us, all gods will disappear." Today, the gods are mythology. When we no longer believe in our own mythological beliefs, they disappear too, and we are no longer the victim of them.

More on this later when we get to the Power of Belief workshop, but we can be a healthy skeptic of our self-limiting beliefs by making use of the following four questions:

1. Is this belief *true or valid*? How so?
2. *How do I react* when I hold this belief – emotionally? Behaviorally?
3. Does this reaction help or *would I be better off* without this belief? How so?
4. What's a *better, more empowering belief* to hold that would help me produce the results I want?

Notice that these four questions are designed to lead to the truth. With rigorous thinking, we can through Questions One, Two, and Three critically challenge our beliefs, determining through logic and data (1) which have validity and which do not, and (2) which are helpful and which are harmful. Then, Question Four leads us to formulate a new self-empowering belief. Through repetition, we can wire a new belief into our heads.

Belief Factor 2: Empowering Affirmations

According to Webster's *American English Dictionary*, an affirmation is an assertion of the truth. This is an interesting definition because in the field of motivational speaking there often is little concern for truth telling. The emphasis is on positive self-talk with little attention to veracity, but self-talk that only propels one to act.

Considered as an affirmation of truth, empowering affirmations possess integrity in that (1) they accurately represent reality, and (2) they create positive action leading to positive results. Consider the difference between these two statements: "I am deeply and fully committed to using every last ounce of my talents to make this book a reality," versus, "I am a brilliant, creative writer whom the public will come to adore." Or, "Writing this book will be difficult, but I can stand all the hardships and hassles along the way," versus, "There is a divine plan for good to come from this work." Notice that the second of these sets of affirmations, while uplifting, are made-up falsehoods designed to trick me into feeling good and/or acting positively. They are not only unprovable, but, worse, lies. The first ones tell the truth, yet are still empowering. It is true that I deeply want to create and am fully committed to creating this book; and, though this book will pose difficulties, I can and will work through them. The bottom line: I find inspiration in these statements without sacrificing my integrity.

I must mention at this point that there is an ugly fact of human nature. We humans find it easy to bombard ourselves with negative affirmations. In fact, I have concluded through my decades of clinical work that rational thinking is not innate. We humans tend to find it just as easy to think irrationally as rationally, to choose fiction over fact, and to adopt negativity over reality.

In the face of this, it makes good sense for a person to build empowering affirmations into the fabric of his or her everyday thinking. Here are a few examples. Please feel free to alter them to fit your situation, and, of course, feel free to create any affirmations that spur you to action.

- "This is important work. Through it, I can make a wonderful contribution."
- "Go for it. The worst that will happen is that I'll fail. I can always learn from it and use the feedback to get one step closer to success."
- "Life is about doing."
- "One step at a time will eventually get me to my goal."

THE POWER OF BELIEF WORKSHOP

I remember years ago addressing a Rotary Club on the Power of Belief. In the question-and-answer session that followed, a gentleman asked, "This is all interesting, but how do we translate it into practical use?"

Good question, I thought. Here's how I answered. "Let me ask you: How many of you spend daily time doing aerobic exercise to keep yourselves physically fit and healthy?"

To my surprise, virtually every one of the 50 or so people in the audience raised their hands.

"Wow," I said, "Congratulations." "But," I went on, "let me ask another question: How many of you spend regular time thinking about your thinking – that is, reflecting on your habitual thought patterns, your basic premises or assumptions about yourself and your life, your deeply held beliefs, paradigms, or philosophies?"

Not surprisingly, no one raised a hand. On a roll, I then went on to talk about how important it is to spend regular time thinking critically about one's own thinking so as not to get mired in self-limiting beliefs and negative affirmations. As my dad used to tell me, you indeed need a sound mind in a sound body.

What follows is the workshop I would have given these Rotarians had I had the time. This one will most likely be more challenging than the earlier one in this chapter. You clinicians, consultants, and coaches would be wise to take a hands-on approach with your clients in processing this one. You laypeople will want to take your time, be thoughtful, and be rigorous. And please don't hesitate to consult with a professional if you get stuck. After all, your success may very well depend on the quality of your performance in this workshop.

Step One: Identify Your Great Results

As with the prior workshop, this one also starts with identifying what great results you are committed to accomplishing. One for me would be to complete this book and get it into the hands of the people who could profit from it. Another would be to raise my younger son Gabriel and my older son Todd to be of high character and competence. Yours can be anything you want, large or small, so long as they are important to you. So, below, list up to three great results you intend to produce. State them positively.

1. _____

_____

_____

_____

2. _____

_____

_____

_____

3. _____
_____
_____
_____

Step Two: Find Your Killer Bs

Remembering the ABC model, identify any Killer Bs that might hold you back from devoting your precious time and energy to making your great results a reality. These are the dragons that need slaying. Look specifically for low frustration tolerance, negativity, self-doubt, perfectionism, and resentment Bs. Put them into complete sentence form, as if you thought them consciously and clearly exactly this way.

Great Results	Killer Bs
1. _____	1. _____
2. _____	2. _____
3. _____	3. _____

Step Three: Subject Your Killer Bs to Healthy Skepticism

Your Step Three goal is to thoughtfully think through the validity of your Killer Bs until you can clearly see their absurdity. Take each of your self-limiting beliefs in turn and challenge them with the following four questions. Much quality thought should be devoted here, as these beliefs are your mortal enemy, and you need to deeply know both how absurd and how self-defeating they are.

Killer Bs: _____
_____
_____
_____

Is this belief true or valid? How so? _____

_____

_____

_____

_____

How do I react when I hold this belief – emotionally? Behaviorally? _____

_____

_____

_____

_____

Does this reaction help me or would I be better off without this belief? How
so? _____

_____

_____

_____

_____

What's a better, more empowering belief to hold that would help me produce
the results I want? _____

_____

_____

_____

_____

Step Four: Develop Empowering Affirmations

Notice how the last question of Step Three leads you to identify a new belief
designed to empower you to act constructively in the service of your great
results. Step Four, then, builds on this by developing your own empowering
affirmations. With thought, write below up to three affirmations you can use to
counter your Killer Bs and stimulate enthusiastic action. Be sure to create them
with integrity.

1. _____

_____

_____

_____

2. _____

_____

_____

_____

3. _____

_____

_____

_____

Step Five: Review and Revise Action Plan

Never leave any workshop without an action plan you can put to immediate use. I suggest at the least that you designate a time each day to think about your thinking, even if you do not do the full workshop each day. Nevertheless, I also suggest that you do the full workshop (1) no less than once a week, and (2) whenever you are stuck or blocked in your efforts.

My implementation plan: _____

_____

_____

_____

_____

When and where I will critically review my plan: _____

_____

_____

_____

_____

Great job! Along with your Power of Focus workshop, you now are well on your way to developing Mental Muscle. As I stated, the more you engage in the content of these workshops, the more habitual your helpful thought patterns will become and the more deeply the self-enhancing beliefs will become ingrained. You will reap the benefits. See for yourself.

INTENSIFIERS

I now offer three tips to help intensify Mental Muscle. If they are used avidly and routinely, you will without doubt greatly strengthen your ability to produce your great results.

Be a Negative Belief Bounty Hunter

Whether by the hand of God, through the evolutionary process, or as the result of just plain old luck, we humans are blessed with the gift of conceptual thought. Virtually everything we find glorious in life – our ability to experience love, our sense of humor, our facility with language, and our ability to appreciate art and music, to name but a few – emanates from this ability to think abstractly.

But there is a problem, a sort of cosmic joke, if you will, that has been played on us. While enjoying this gift of conceptual thought, we do not possess the ability to use it very well. As stated earlier in this chapter, the human mind finds it just as easy to think irrationally, magically, and fancifully as it does rationally, factually, and realistically, thereby regularly prompting us to react in self-defeating ways.

If what I've just stated is accurate, it makes sense to become a negative belief bounty hunter. You would be wise to reserve a few minutes each day to track down and do violence to your self-limiting beliefs. The format that I have found exceptionally helpful is to start each day by (1) previewing important tasks and situations to be faced before bedtime, (2) identifying any Killer Bs you may harbor about the tasks, (3) challenging each of them using the four questions posed earlier, and (4) replacing them with better ones.

You may use any format that works for you. But please, please, please do not let a negative belief fester for even a day.

An Apple a Day

One of the more cogent remarks I have heard was voiced by a music teacher who attended one of my Mental Muscle workshops. She pithily said, "If I don't set the tone for my day, then other people and circumstances will."

I couldn't agree more. If we don't take the time to establish the mindset we want at the start of each and every day, we could easily fall into negativity. What better way to do this than with empowering affirmations. For those of you who think you have little time to do this, I say, nonsense. There are multiple opportunities – for example, while shaving, in the shower, or driving to work – where a few minutes of "attitude adjustment" can do wonders. Just as an apple a day keeps the doctor away, an empowering affirmation a day keeps self-defeating behaviors at bay.

Practice, Practice, Practice

There is an old adage that says the best way to get to perform at Carnegie Hall is to practice, practice, practice. We know that this is just as true for developing Mental Muscle as it is for musical ability. Not only do skills of mental focus and self-helpful thinking get ingrained with practice, but we have also found that neurological connections actually get formed in the brain.

If we can become at least half as good at leveraging pleasure and pain, harnessing rewards and punishments, eradicating self-limiting beliefs, and developing empowering affirmations as their opposite, we will notice enormous, positive change. Remember that tendencies toward negative thinking never take a day off, not even on Sundays and holidays. So, practicing each day the four Mental Muscle strategies will both keep the wolves away and keep us on track to producing your great results.

AN ORGANIZATIONAL CASE STUDY

Drive-killing thinking will cripple any organization's ability to succeed to its fullest. Take the example of a local business facing a significant downsizing, the employee body being wracked with anxiety because no one knew whether they'd continue to have a job or not. Imagine the toll this took on their focus, their drive, and their productivity.

To start the day-long workshop, I leveled with them by acknowledging the grim reality of their situation and expressing my regret that they had to face this. I went on to emphasize that, while I had no power to change the downsizing situation within their company, I could help them deal with it without being traumatized. I invited them to work with me to develop the Mental Muscle to deal gracefully with the current situation and to work constructively to find another job should they be one of the unlucky people to be laid off.

In the service of building Mental Muscle, I then launched into an explanation of the Power of Belief (see pp. 101–107), peppering my lecture with examples from my clinical practice. I worked mightily to convey its core:

- They, the workforce, suffered from not one, but two problems: first, the practical problem of their job threat and, second, their disempowering stressful reactions.
- They may not have had a whole lot of control over their future at their company, but they had total control over their reaction to the situation.
- It was not the Activating Event (the A) of possibly losing their jobs that caused the emotional Consequences (the C) of their anxiety, but the Killer Beliefs (the B) that they held that caused it.
- More specifically, they caused their stress and anxiety by virtue of holding and actively endorsing one or more of the five Killer Bs: LFT, negativity, self-doubt, perfectionism, and/or resentment.
- To eliminate their anxiety, thus freeing them to focus on both being productive at their job while employed and working effectively to secure another job if laid off, they had best identify, dispute, and replace their Killer Bs.

The workshop really caught fire once it moved from me laying the conceptual groundwork to the change phase. In this phase, I demonstrated with three volunteers what they needed to do to gain Mental Muscle, the first being Karen. After identifying her low frustration tolerance, negativity, and self-doubting Killer Bs, I led her to skeptically discredit them. Here is an approximation of the conversation we had in front of all the participants:

Dr. G.:   So, Karen, is it really true or valid that losing your job would be so horrible that your life would be virtually over?

Karen: It sure feels like it.

Dr. G.:   But, is it, really? What could you do if you unfortunately lost your job?

Karen: I guess I could stay at my parents' for a while.

Dr. G.:   Okay, so, you have people to help you out. You're not alone, you won't starve to death. Now, what about finding another job?

Karen: That'd be hard.

Dr. G.:   I know, but hard only means hard, not impossible. Would it be impossible?

Karen: I guess not. I suppose I could find something, sooner or later.

Dr. G.:   Exactly. You could go live with your parents and work your fanny off each day to find another job, even if it took a whole year, couldn't you?

Karen: Yes.

Dr. G.:   So it's not the end of the world to lose this job; it's just a short-term hardship that's fixable – that is, if you stick with finding a new job till you get one. Yes?

Karen: Yes.

Dr. G.:   And, by the way, how do you react when you hold onto all these negative, catastrophizing beliefs?

Karen: I don't know – I can't sleep, I walk around with a burning in my chest. I'm just miserable.

Dr. G.:   And how self-defeating is it to think those ways? What about your productivity?

Karen: I can't concentrate. I have no desire to work or do much of anything.

Dr. G.:   Even preparing your résumé, checking the newspaper for other jobs, and so on?

Karen: You nailed me.

Dr. G.:   So it's clear you'd be a whole lot better off getting rid of those irrational beliefs. They not only make you miserable, but also rob you of your get up and go. Now, what's a better, more empowering way to think?

Karen: I guess it would be something like this. I sure don't want to lose this job, but, if I did, the world wouldn't come to an end. It may be rough for a while, but I'll be okay and I'll eventually find another job.

Dr. G.:   Excellent! Now, how do you feel thinking that way?

Karen: Better. More relaxed. Confident.

Dr. G.:   Good. Now, the last step is to develop an action plan for you to rehearse your new, empowering beliefs till they become automatic.

Once I finished with Karen, I reviewed the five steps of the Power of Belief workshop (pp. 107–112) and conducted two more demonstrations, followed by discussion and instruction. For the rest of the day, I broke the participants down into triads to help each other through the Power of Belief workshop, the end product being a powerful action plan to stay calm and be productive.

I am happy to report the success of this consultative effort. Two-hour follow-up sessions each of the next three months showed a workforce adhering to their belief plans, less anxious, and more productive. Mission accomplished.

I want to add that those in leadership roles would be wise to do all they can do to build Mental Muscle into their workforce. Here are some concrete steps that can be taken:

- Provide Mental Muscle training to all employees. Remember: even the most skillful people in the world are rendered inept when emotionally contaminated by negative, irrational thinking.
- Make sure the workforce is populated by positive-thinking people. To say it another way, eliminate as quickly as possible those employees who are

entrenched negative thinkers because they will not be able to devote themselves to furthering your organization's results and will likely contaminate others' thinking as well.

- Take pains to keep people focused on the organization's Passionate Purpose or mission, as well as on its vision of its ideal future. This could be done in concrete ways such as: displaying the Mission Statements throughout the building; connecting the relevance of the organizational Passionate Purpose to both the strategic plan and to each individual's role in the success of the entire enterprise; and making the employee's contribution to the organizational Passionate Purpose part of the annual review process.

- Avoid the criticism trap. Too often, those in supervisory or management positions expect perfection and only give feedback when a person errs. The end result is that employees receive little praise and only criticism. This can lead not only to hurt feelings, but also to discouragement, a rupture in their identification with the organization, and destroyed drive. The mantra should be: catch them doing good and let them know it.

- Those in leadership roles should regularly dispense rewards to all employees. At a minimum, each employee should get a verbal recognition at least once a week.

- Institute the WIIFM – What's In It For Me – principle. As with my patient Bob, whom I described earlier in this chapter, each employee should be helped to see the profound personal benefits (pleasures) in doing quality work and the debilitating personal costs (pains) of failing to do so. When a person is clear about their WIIFM, he or she is more likely to be strong-minded and produce results.

- Identify and destroy negative thinking. Sometimes, negative thinking is embedded in the organizational culture as, for example, the belief held by most everyone in a small construction company: "We're just the little guy on the block." Their beliefs will spread like wildfire throughout the employee body, and they will curtail the boldness and drive needed for extraordinary results.

A FINAL WORD

Our mind is the center of who we are. It houses not only our store of knowledge, but, more importantly, our values, our deepest desires, our self-concept, and our most honored beliefs, philosophies, and paradigms. All these drive us to show up each day in life as we do.

Given the supreme significance of our mind in having both a happy and a successful life, we would be remiss to not purposely develop those qualities of mind that give us a leg up in creating the great results we want. The two legs of Mental Muscle – the Power of Focus and the Power of Belief – are yours to build, if only you will do so. This chapter gives the backdrop and the strategies. It's up to each of us to take advantage of them. The opportunity for greatness is there. Go for it.

REFERENCES AND SUGGESTED READING

Bach, R. (1989). *The illusions of a reluctant messiah.* New York: Dell Publishing.

Carlson, R. (1997). *Don't sweat the small stuff ... and it's all small stuff.* New York: Hyperion.

Carnegie, D. (1984). *How to stop worrying and start living.* New York: Simon & Schuster.

Ellis, A., & Harper, R. A. (1997). *A guide to rational living.* Hollywood, CA: Wilshire Book Company.

Epictetus (1948). *The enchiridion.* Indianapolis, IN: The Bobbs-Merrill Company.

Homer (1992). *The iliad.* London: Penguin.

Katie, B. (2002). *Loving who one is: four questions that can change your life.* New York: Harmony Books.

Ruiz, D. M. (1997). *The four agreements.* San Rafael, CA: Amber-Allen Publishing.

Skinner, B. F. (1974). *About behaviorism.* New York: Alfred A. Knopf.

Zilbergeld, B., & Lazarus, A. A. (1987). *Mind power.* Boston, MA: Little, Brown & Company.

CHAPTER 7

Robust Vitality

Building high, sustained energy – physical, mental, and emotional

> *This is the single most powerful investment we can ever make in our life –*
> *investment in ourselves.*
> Stephen Covey

My wife and I own a small cottage in the United States Virgin Islands. As much of the island is jungle-like, the multitude of centipedes, termites, and scorpions that co-exist with us can make life uncomfortable if uncontrolled. To keep these creatures at bay, we contract a pest control service to periodically spray our property. If you think about it, Sandra, the owner of the service, has a wonderful job. For starters, she lives in the Caribbean. Moreover, she drives between appointments gazing at nothing but gorgeous views. Maybe best of all, she can take a dip at any one of the many majestic beaches at lunchtime or at the end of her workday.

I'm sure you'd be tempted to trade places with Sandra if given the chance. But, listen to the following conversation she and I had when she dropped by for her last inspection:

Sandra: I see you're offering a stress management seminar for business people next week. I sure wish I could attend.

Dr. G.:   Well, I hope you make it.

Sandra: Unfortunately, I'm too busy.

Dr. G.:   What's going on? Business too good?

Sandra: You don't know the half of it. I work all the time – six days a week at this job, then Sundays are for laundry, bathrooms, and other chores at home.

Dr. G.:   Wow. You sure are a busy, busy person.

Sandra: I'm up at 4.30 a.m. and off to the gym. That's my only time to exercise. I get home by 6.00, walk the dog, get the kids off to school, and I'm at work by 7.30. I work all day until 6.00 or 7.00 at night, pull

supper together, and then drop into bed exhausted by 9.00 to face
another day just the same.

Dr. G.:   Whew! All that must take quite a toll on you.

Sandra: I'm fatigued. I have a kind of exhaustion of the soul, a sense of just
going through the motions. I don't know how long I can keep this
up.

How many times do we find ourselves in Sandra's shoes, overloaded with
responsibilities, pushing ourselves to the limit, finding little if any time to take
care of ourselves? We may keep on top of our business, and even achieve some
success, but we pay the price physically, mentally, and emotionally.

Too many of us find little time for rest, renewal, and rejuvenation. Without
carving out this time, our reserves can easily get depleted. Like Sandra, we can
easily become dull and burnt out, stressed, irritable, low in energy, and diminished
in passion. Finding ways to keep ourselves energized – full of Robust Vitality – is
absolutely critical to keeping alive the Unrelenting Drive, Dedication, and
Determination necessary for making our great results a reality.

Following Stephen Covey's quote at the top of this chapter, the most important
investment we can make is the investment in ourselves. This chapter will provide
a workable template to do just that: strategies to create and maintain Robust
Vitality in order to bring energy and passion to each day.

THE THREE DIMENSIONS OF ROBUST VITALITY

The path to Robust Vitality comes in many forms. However, it seems proper to
organize them into three fundamental categories: (1) physical vitality; (2) mental
vitality; and (3) emotional vitality. In this chapter, I will address all three. For each,
I will make a handful of suggestions that, if implemented, will escalate anyone's
vitality. The goal is to grow all three dimensions in a reasoned, balanced way.

Physical Vitality

My dad used to preach to me an Ancient Greek principle, "A sound mind in a
sound body." About physical vitality, you might want to pose this question: Do
I experience vitality and energy most every day, or do I often feel tired, worn out,
and depleted? If your answer leans to the latter, you would be wise to focus on
increasing your physical vitality.

Here are four common sense, yet powerful strategies to help you increase
your energy. The purpose is not to post the best time in the 10K or look as good
in a bathing suit as when in high school. Rather, the purpose is to maximize your
vitality in order to help produce your desired great results.

1. **Exercise regularly.** We all know that exercise is good for us. It burns calories, accelerates heart rate, thereby warding off coronary artery disease, and strengthens our body. Yet, not being professional athletes with a need to push ourselves to the limit, exercise for our purpose is to increase energy and vitality.

   Here are six suggestions to help you increase your physical vitality:

   • Incorporate all three components of exercise into your routine: (1) aerobic exercise for endurance; (2) stretching for flexibility; and (3) resistance for strength.

   • Be moderate in your exercise. Remember that you are neither a teenager nor an Olympian. I can attest to the fact that the "no pain, no gain" perspective is a sure-fire formula for injury. So, set moderate goals, ones that give you a workout, but do not overly strain, stress, or fatigue you.

   • Be sure to warm up and cool down. Before launching into your routine, stretch each and every muscle group you will use in your workout. Also begin your exercise at a very slow pace and gradually pick up speed; to ignore this will invite injuries that can put you on the shelf for days if not weeks. Be alert to how your body reacts during your workout; if you feel any strain or pain, slow down or stop entirely. Finally, cool down after your workout by walking for a few minutes and then again do your stretching. Here is a stretching tip: a few seconds of stretching will loosen up your muscles, but a full two-minute stretch will over time permanently stretch those muscles.

   • Make exercise fun. The rewards you get from exercise are as much a function of the pleasure it provides as the physical benefits themselves. Find activities you enjoy. Exercise with companions. Listen to music or books on tape while working out. If you don't enjoy it, you will likely end up quitting.

   • Reward yourself for your effort, not your performance. Remember that success is measured by your vitality rather than your speed or number of reps.

   • Above all, keep in mind the purpose of your exercise routine. The purpose is to increase your physical vitality so that you can sustain the energy needed to produce great results.

2. **Get sufficient rest.** As with many men of a certain age, I suffered from a benign condition that caused me to awake several times each night. It was only after I had this condition repaired that I was once again able to enjoy a full night of uninterrupted sleep. I was amazed not only at how good I then felt, but also how tired and depleted I had gotten used to feeling from my previous lack of sufficient sleep.

Here are some tips to help you make best use of your sleep:

- Early to bed, early to rise. My college basketball coach used to preach that one hour of sleep before midnight is worth two afterwards. I don't know if this is actually true, but I do know that getting to bed early gives one time to exercise in the morning (when it's most beneficial), makes it so you don't have to rush to start the day, and gives you time to connect with your loved ones before going off to work.
- Just after turning out the light at night, meditate on positive, pleasant, reassuring thoughts: "I'm safe and secure," "Everything is good and fine," and, if religious, "I'm in God's hands." These are the type of thoughts that help bring that peace of mind that aids sound sleep. As the song says, count your blessings instead of sheep.
- Be careful to not take on stimulating or worrisome pursuits the hour or two before bedtime. These will only serve to rile you up, a sure-fire formula for rumination rather than sleep.
- Make peace with your significant others before retiring for the night. Taking hurt, anger, and/or apprehension to bed with you will both make it difficult to peacefully drift off and almost certainly make a restful night impossible.
- Do not put pressure on yourself to go to sleep. Thinking things like "I have to get to sleep" or "I'll be dead tired tomorrow if I don't nod off quickly" will be counterproductive. Take the attitude "While I want a great night's sleep, it's OK if I don't; the worst is that I'll be tired tomorrow, which won't kill me." This perspective takes the pressure off and, if truly believed, will help you fall asleep. If nothing works, read something enjoyable, listen to relaxing music, or make use of the time you have by doing something constructive. Tomorrow night is another night.

3. **Eat the right kind of food, in moderate amounts, and in the proper sequence.** This pretty much tells it all. I am not a nutritionist, but I will make a few suggestions that will immensely enrich your vitality:

- Follow the King, Queen, Pauper strategy. Most of us consume food backwards, by eating our biggest meal at supper. To the contrary, the king of meals ought to be breakfast in order to give us all the energy we need for the day. Then, eat a moderate, queen-sized lunch, and finally a lightweight pauper meal for dinner.
- Drink plenty of water throughout the day. Different people recommend different amounts, but my goal is eight eight-ounce glasses each day. This amount keeps me hydrated, keeps my kidneys

active and clean, and tends to keep my stomach feeling full so there's little temptation to snack. Besides, water is vital to the brain and sparks me up mentally.

- Snack on fruits and vegetables instead of cookies, peanuts, chips, or ice cream. There is an amazing variety of fruits and vegetables, enough to satisfy any taste. Experiment and you will see that I'm right.
- Reduce your processed food intake. Be sure you peruse the labels before you purchase food. If a food is high in salt content, has five ingredients you can't pronounce, and is high in calories, cholesterol, or total fat, do not buy it. A simple rule of thumb is: buy fresh, buy local, and stay out of the middle of the grocery store as the best food tends to be on the outer edges.
- Make a point to leave the table a tiny bit hungry. The Japanese model is to be four-fifths full, and the Germans say, "Tie up the sack before it's full."

4. **Eliminate damaging habits.** Your primary care physician will be the first to warn you that a very high percentage of all diseases are caused by lifestyle choices. Poor lifestyle choices not only rob one of vitality but can also literally lead to premature death. Some of the more pernicious lifestyle choices are the following:

- coffee and caffeine, which are artificial stimulants that become craved because vitality is already lacking;
- cigarettes, which are the cause of over 420,000 deaths each year in the United States alone;
- alcohol and drugs, the abuse of which not only destroys health, but happiness, careers, and families as well.

As a practicing clinical psychologist, I can confidently assert that these damaging habits are psychologically driven. They grow out of a need for immediate gratification and/or the desperate drive to eliminate any discomfort one may feel. In their stronger forms, they can be an addiction or a compulsion. If you struggle with any of these bad habits, I strongly urge the following:

- Eliminate denial. That is, freely admit that you have a self-defeating habit that undercuts your vitality.
- My dad used to say that quitting smoking was easy; after all, he did it over a hundred times. Because habit breaking is so difficult, you might consider seeking professional help. This does not mean that you are a weak or disturbed individual. It only means that you most likely could benefit from the assistance of a professional who is

trained to assist you in erasing the underlying cognitions and emotions that often drive these self-defeating habits.
- Seek support from trusted peers. Research on smoking cessation shows us that a combination of medical assistance in the form of prescription patches and a support group is most effective. Have at least one trusted person to support you, cheerlead for you, and even help block you when temptation strikes.

Mental Vitality

A close friend of mine is the poster child for mental vitality. Finding himself living alone in his 40s and free to make his own schedule, he decided to awake at 5 a.m. to treat himself to two solid hours of substantive reading before beginning his workday.

Hal recently told me that he has sustained this habit now for almost three decades. I can honestly report that it is a delight to sit and talk with him. In addition to supplying friendly, guy-type banter, he is a font of interesting, provocative, and even wise bits of information gleaned from his readings.

The sad fact is that Hal is the exception rather than the rule. Rather than continue to grow ourselves mentally, most of us neglect to stimulate our minds once formal education is behind us.

What about you? Are you Hal-like or average-Joe-like? Do you regularly devote time to learn new ideas and acquire new perspectives? Do you devote yourself to keeping your mind stimulated or do you mentally stagnate?

However you answered these questions, here are five straightforward ideas for you to increase your mental vitality. Again, the purpose is not to raise your IQ or make you look more learned to your friends and colleagues, but to help you hone the organ that is probably most important to making your great results a reality.

1. **Read good literature.** I appreciate the value of light reading for relaxation. At the same time, good literature provides many wonderful additional opportunities, including: (1) excitement and pleasure in exploring new, perhaps provocative ideas and information; (2) exposure to new perspectives, ones you probably would never come to on your own; (3) a tremendous resource for practical information, skills, and tools to put to immediate use; (4) an ability to converse knowledgably with a wider array of people; (5) access to what learned people have taught about contending with the vicissitudes of life; (6) a perspective on how important events from the past connect to what you experience in your present life; and (7) ideas and strategies to help to lead a happy, productive life.

Bookstores and libraries are so full of fascinating reading material that you couldn't get through all the possibilities in two lifetimes. One obvious resource is outstanding works of fiction; these not only serve to entertain, but they often also explore values, perspectives, and other critical nuances of the human condition. Other resources are: biographies, memoirs, and autobiographies; philosophical treatises; historical material; self-help and spiritual tomes; instructional books on every subject under the sun; political thoughts; relationship enhancement teachings; and a whole lot more.

2. **Write.** Similar to reading, writing has the power to keep our mind vibrant. Writing letters (as opposed to cryptic text messages), keeping a journal or a diary, composing position papers on topics you find interesting, crafting professional papers or articles, and writing personal memoir pieces are all examples of mental activities that can help you both organize your thoughts and keep your mind alive as well.

3. **Do crossword puzzles.** My mom always had a crossword puzzle handy. Except for esoteric bits of information from the world of science or literature, she rarely needed any help to complete the puzzles. I cannot prove this, but I am pretty sure that this habit was significant in her being sharp as a tack when she died at the ripe old age of 93.

4. **Continue your education.** Recent surveys show that the television is on in most homes anywhere from 35 to 45 hours per week. Although I have no data to support it, my guess is that most of these hours are spent on fairly mindless programs such as soap operas, comedy shows, and night-time dramas, not the science, discovery or history channels.

Classes, seminars, and workshops are invaluable vehicles to continually hone and expand the mind. Most every city has organizations that offer learning opportunities, as for example public libraries, bookstores, community colleges, continuing education departments of universities and colleges, the Chamber of Commerce, and individuals who simply want to share a body of knowledge or skill with others.

An acquaintance of mine determined not to stagnate once he retired. He became almost obsessive about his continuing education. So far, he has attended courses in Civil War history (a fertile area for study here in Virginia), acting, sign language, auto mechanics, speaking Italian, a survey of the great classical composers, and the basics of playing the guitar. Granted he has a ton of spare time, but he sure works hard to keep his mind keen. You can do so too.

5. **Organize and plan.** Simply reacting to whatever arises during the day reflects in some ways a lazy mind. A vibrant person is one who systematically works to achieve his or her goals. Thoreau tells us, "It is not enough to be busy; so are the ants. The question is: what are we

busy about?" (Thoreau, n.d.)To which I add a follow-up question: "Are you organized, systematic, and foresightful about that with which you are busy?"

Emotional Vitality

I think it true that everyone from time to time faces adversity. For some lucky few, the adversities are minor and infrequent. For most of us, though, adversity comes in many shapes and sizes and shows up all too frequently. In addition to the run-of-the-mill ones, sooner or later we are likely to face such life difficulties as financial strains, career setbacks, physical infirmities, conflicted or impaired relationships, and the death of loved ones.

Either way, every last one of us will face adversity. And, as Ben Sherwood points out in his excellent book *The Survivors Club* (2009), when you experience adversity, it is not all relative. When adversity strikes – when it happens in your life, right here and now, threatening you in some way – it is a big deal to you, and your challenge is just as daunting to you as is anyone else's. Yet, in the face of life's challenges, some people seem to emotionally sail along, keeping their chin up, living fully. In contrast, others fall into the morass of crippling bitterness, self-pity, and/or depression. They thereby not only suffer emotionally, but they also find it difficult to summon the focus and energy to persist in the pursuit of their great results.

From my more than 35 years of clinical practice, I have observed that what determines how well one responds to adversity (and more generally the degree to which one leads a happy, fulfilled life) depends on how attentive and intelligent one is to sustaining emotional vitality. So, I ask you, are you generally happy and fulfilled, or do you find yourself frequently frustrated, disgruntled, and unhappy? Do you keep adversity in perspective, or do you overreact to the hardships you face? Do you plug away when facing adversity, or are you being held back from meeting your goals because of the contamination of anger, guilt, or depression?

What follows are seven elegant strategies to help you grow both your emotional stability and vitality. As with any other skill, there is a learning curve. The more you practice these, the better you will get at them, and the more emotionally vital you will be.

1. **Live your Passionate Purpose.** As emphasized in Chapter 3, having a Passionate Purpose will energize you in several ways: (1) you will experience a sense of meaning to your life; (2) you will be primed to figure out how to express your Passionate Purpose in each of your day's activities, thereby enriching even the most mundane task; (3) you will perceive your life as important regardless of your station; (4) you will become more focused and disciplined and less responsive to the

immediate, trivial temptations that can distract you from your great results; (5) you will persist in the pursuit of your great goals because they are in the service of your Passionate Purpose; (6) you likely will be more productive and successful in your life; (7) you will have great satisfaction each and every day, for, after all, you are doing meaningful things; and (8) you will take great pride in your accomplishments.

A life filled with personal meaning not only provides deep pleasure and even joy, but also (1) insulates us from overreacting to adversity, (2) fills us with emotional vitality, and (3) drives us to achieve our great results. So, creating your Passionate Purpose and acting on it is one of the best strategies for emotional vitality.

2. **Focus on contributing.** As stated earlier, if each of us would go home each night and be good to those with whom we live, we would transform the world. Those who experience our love and respect would be more prone to feel happy, be more self-accepting, and be more trusting of others. They then would, as a result, be more likely to give the same to others so that, after a while, we would have a global ripple effect.

   Maybe I am much too idealistic about the human race. What I do know, though, is that we are strengthened when we focus on contributing to the well-being of the people who pass through our lives, especially when we do this with no expectations for receiving in return. Do I advocate monk-like self-sacrifice or an obliteration of our own wants and desires? Absolutely not. What I do advocate, however, is habituating ourselves to these kinds of questions: What contribution can I make to the health and happiness of my loved ones today? What can I do to serve my clients or customers better today? How can I enrich the experience of the friend I encounter for lunch today? How can I make the life of each and every person I pass today just a little more pleasant? Try asking and, of course, acting on these type of questions and see how it affects your emotional vitality.

3. **Plan for fun.** High-vitality people have the same day-to-day grinds as others, but they manage to build enjoyable and rewarding activities into the fabric of their days. Even amidst the Cuban Missile Crisis, President Kennedy squeezed in his daily swim and several informal dinners with close friends. He surely knew that all work and no play would make John a dull boy.

   We all find fun in different activities, of course, but if you inject a bit of fun into your routine, you emotional vitality will soar. Here are two tips:

   • Schedule some small activity that gives you pleasure each day (e.g., listening to music, dancing, reading a book, a short walk, a hot bath, a phone chat with a dear friend, a cup of hot chocolate, and on and on).

- Always have some big adventure on the horizon to which to look forward (e.g., a concert, a weekend trip to the beach, a vacation, a special birthday or anniversary celebration, a golfing trip to Pinehurst, or wherever your heart desires).

4. **Lighten up.** The late, great psychologist Dr. Albert Ellis once noted that the essence of all emotional disturbances is taking oneself and life too seriously. For it is when people think that they have to do everything perfectly and be universally applauded, that others must always treat them well, and that life has to always work out the way they want that they sooner or later become anxious, angry, and/or depressed. These are pretty serious, even life-or-death ways to think, aren't they?

   What better way to ward off debilitating emotional states than to lighten up? The truth is that while we naturally desire to do well, be treated well, and have life always work out the way we want, it is hardly ever life or death. Taking a more lighthearted approach to life, even seeing the humor in things, can go a long way to keeping ourselves emotionally vital. Remember what Proverbs 17:22 tells us: "A cheerful heart is good medicine."

5. **Follow the Serenity Prayer.** You are probably familiar with the wonderful little prayer crafted by the philosopher Reinhold Niebuhr (1987, p. 251):

   > God grant me the serenity to accept the things I cannot change, the courage to change the things I can and the wisdom to know the difference.

What a wonderful philosophy. Millions of people have found wisdom in this simple prayer to aid in their recovery from some addictive substance. Lore has it that the former Major League Baseball player Mickey Rivers put it into his own words when he said:

> Ain't no sense worrying about things you can control, because if you can control it, there's no sense worrying. And there ain't no sense worrying about things you can't control, because if you can't control it, there ain't no sense worrying. (Rivers and DeMarco, 2003, p. 104)

So, when you face adversity, ask yourself whether or not you can control it. If you can, figure out how and do it. But, if you have decided you can't control a negative situation, you might as well not waste your time worrying. Instead, work on accepting the unpleasant adversity you unfortunately have in your life without protest or catastrophizing and move on.

6. **Practice enlightened self-interest.** Many of us get caught in the trap of putting everyone and everything else first. We get it pounded into our heads that it is noble to give, to sacrifice, to look out for the other guy, even if it is detrimental to our own well-being. Being socialized to nurture and care for others, women are most vulnerable to this cult of self-sacrifice.

But look at the costs. By being self-sacrificing, we often find ourselves giving up what satisfies us. We can then become frustrated, bitter, and stressed. We end up with nothing left, not only for ourselves, but for anyone else as well.

Enlightened self-interest starts from the premise that no one is put on this earth to make our life work. By the age of 18 or so, it is our responsibility, not our spouse's, our friends', or our colleagues'. Therefore, while putting at least a select few others a very close second so that we do not act selfishly, we hold ourselves just a little bit more important to ourselves than we do others. We do not say that we are more important or better than they are, but that they are a tad less important to us than we are to us. We thereby are primed to look after our own interests without being either self-sacrificing or selfish.

Armed with the philosophy of enlightened self-interest, you are now free to act on the following:

- Make sure you know what is important to you.
- When confronted with a decision about what to do, ask yourself: Does doing this aid and abet what's important to me – my values, desires, and interests – or does it thwart me in some important way? If the latter, decline to do it, unless it does severe damage to others.
- Assert yourself to say "No" when you truly don't want to do something.
- Balance your life with a healthy mixture of doing for yourself and also doing for others.
- Build in self-renewal and self-pleasurable activities as a natural by-product of the fact that you are a legitimate, important member of the human race.
- Simplify your life by ridding it of things that are unimportant to you or that you feel pressure to perform because they are important to others.

7. **Stamp out ego.** As discussed in Chapter 4, a sure-fire way to create emotional distress is to tie your human worth to your performances. This is the essence of ego, one of the most pernicious concepts ever invented.

Strive mightily to distinguish your performances from your Self. For example, I do psychology, but I am not a psychologist; I write, but I am not a writer; I consult with businesses and organizations, but I am not a consultant.

Then, with this distinction in mind, you can, if you want, rate how well or badly you perform. But, you do not rate as good or bad your essence or your Self. Thus, I do psychology well, but that does not make me a good person; I fail to run marathons, but that hardly qualifies me as a failure as a person; I succeed quite well at times as a business consultant but fall short at other times, but, regardless, I, my Being, is never all good or all bad.

In short, ego comes about when we collapse the distinction between what we do and who we are. Once we draw the distinction and stubbornly refuse to either identify or judge our Selves by what we do or how well we do it, we free ourselves from ego. Without ego, we are then free to just do without fear. We can just enjoy the effort, feeling emotionally vital the whole time.

THE ROBUST VITALITY WORKSHOP

I hope the aforementioned strategies for stoking your Robust Vitality struck you as sound and sensible. I also hope that you were encouraged to continue those you already practice and excited to take on at least a few others that are not presently a part of your repertoire. After all, you must have the fuel you need to power your vehicle down the road.

The following five steps guide you to an action plan to generate the vitality you need to create your great results. I urge you to do this workshop with enthusiasm and commitment.

Step One: Conduct Self-Assessment

Step One asks two things of you. The first is to rate yourself on each of the three dimensions of Robust Vitality. The second is to identify an initial list of activities that would improve your vitality on each of these dimensions. Caution: be careful to not take on more than you can comfortably handle, as you do not want to set yourself up for failure.

Physical Vitality

1. Rate yourself on the four strategies to bring about physical vitality, noting your strengths and weaknesses.

	Poor				Excellent
1. Exercising regularly	1	2	3	4	5
2. Getting sufficient rest	1	2	3	4	5
3. Eating healthily	1	2	3	4	5
4. Eliminating damaging habits	1	2	3	4	5

2. Reflecting on your ratings, make a list of activities that would help you create and sustain physical vitality. These can include things you do not do, things you do infrequently, or even things you already do. These also can include the reduction or elimination of things you do that you would best not do. _____

_____

_____

_____

_____

Mental Vitality

1. Rate yourself on the five strategies to increase your mental vitality. Without denial, note your strengths and weaknesses so as to aid you in your vitality action planning.

	Poor				Excellent
1. Reading good literature	1	2	3	4	5
2. Writing	1	2	3	4	5
3. Doing crossword puzzles	1	2	3	4	5
4. Continuing your education	1	2	3	4	5
5. Organizing and planning	1	2	3	4	5

2. Make a list of activities that you think would increase your mental vitality. What could you start to do? What are you already doing that you would be wise to increase? What would both stimulate you and be fun?

_____

_____

_____

_____

_____

Emotional Vitality

1. Rate yourself on the seven strategies to perk up your emotional vitality. Noting your strengths and weaknesses on these can help you plan improvements.

	Poor				Excellent
1. Living your Passionate Purpose	1	2	3	4	5
2. Focusing on contributing	1	2	3	4	5
3. Planning for fun	1	2	3	4	5
4. Lightening up	1	2	3	4	5
5. Following the Serenity Prayer	1	2	3	4	5
6. Practicing enlightened self-interest	1	2	3	4	5
7. Stamping out ego	1	2	3	4	5

2. Reflect on your emotional vitality self ratings. What would you be wise to start doing? What could you do more of that would increase your zest for life? What would help you be more happy and peaceful? List these below along with any ideas you might have for implementation.

_____

_____

_____

_____

_____

Step Two: Create an Action Plan

From the physical, mental, and emotional activities you identified in Step One, create an action plan to increase your Robust Vitality. Be careful to be realistic. Do not be too ambitious. Do only what you can realistically do. Also, attempt to bring some balance to your plan by paying attention to each dimension. Lastly, be as specific as possible with regard to how often, where, and when.

Vitality Activity	Frequency	Where/When
1. _____	_____	_____
2. _____	_____	_____
3. _____	_____	_____
4. _____	_____	_____

5. _____   _____   _____

6. _____   _____   _____

7. _____   _____   _____

8. _____   _____   _____

Step Three: Eliminate Blocks

The third step is to identify and eliminate those circumstances that block you from acting on your Robust Vitality action plan. These blocks come in two varieties:

1. Outer blocks are those tangible impediments outside your skin. They include any number of things such as an overly packed schedule, family responsibilities, the traffic you encounter during an average day, the weather, and social obligations.
2. Inner blocks are those impediments inside you that have the potential to derail your efforts to achieve vitality. These include your moment-by-moment mood, the state of your present motivation, and whether or not you feel physically hale and hearty.

Any or all of these circumstances have the potential to block you from implementing your Robust Vitality action plan. You have a choice: you can use them as excuses for not following your action plan, or you can eliminate or alter them so that you can follow through on your plan. Remember: it's your choice.

Reflecting across the spectrum of your life, make a comprehensive list of both the outer and inner circumstances you predict might derail your Robust Vitality action plan. For each, devise a strategy to eliminate or bypass that block.

Block	Strategy to Eliminate/Bypass
1. _____	_____
_____	_____
2. _____	_____
_____	_____
3. _____	_____
_____	_____
4. _____	_____
_____	_____
5. _____	_____
_____	_____

Step Four: Reward Yourself

Following through on any new resolve can be a very difficult undertaking. If you are like me, you have crashed and burned on more New Year's resolutions than you can count.

Harkening back to Chapter 6, remember the power of using greatly valued rewards to motivate you to follow through on intended actions. As you will recall, rewarding a behavior greatly increases the likelihood of you doing that behavior in the future.

To make purposeful use of this principle, think first of things you greatly value that you have available every day. For me, these include such things as the morning newspaper, quality time with my wife and son in the evening, my favorite cable news show, various reading materials, and my professional or creative writing. Your rewards can be anything, but they must be valuable to you.

Once you have identified these rewarding items, you need to make enjoying them contingent upon performing the intended vitality action. "Contingent" is the key word; the reward is contingent on the action. For example, you can decide to reward yourself with the morning newspaper for that early morning workout, but only if you do the workout. No workout means no newspaper. Or, you only allow yourself the enjoyment of an evening movie if you follow through on your stimulating reading. If you do not read, you do not get to watch a movie.

Now, create your own reward plan. For each item on your action plan, identify a powerful, valued reward that you will only give to yourself if you do the action. If you do it, you earn the reward; if you do not do it, you forego the reward. Remember that you can always enjoy the reward by simply doing the action. In other words, you never have to deny yourself your reward if you choose to act as intended.

Vitality Activity	Reward
1. _____	_____
2. _____	_____
3. _____	_____
4. _____	_____
5. _____	_____
6. _____	_____
7. _____	_____
8. _____	_____

Step Five: Mobilize Support

As preached throughout this book, it is most beneficial to enlist the help of trusted others in your efforts. They can offer support, coaching, and cheerleading, not to mention tough love and hard feedback.

To complete your Robust Vitality action plan, name the person or persons whom you will ask to support you, as well as exactly what you will ask them to do on your behalf. The more specific your request as to what you want from them, the more likely they are to give you the support you want.

	Support Person(s)	Request
1.	_____	_____
2.	_____	_____
3.	_____	_____

INTENSIFIERS

Congratulations on the superb job you did on your Robust Vitality workshop. But, remember that you will not reap the benefits without sustained follow-through. To intensify your Robust Vitality, here are three additional strategies you could incorporate into your routine.

Get Rid of All "Have-Tos"

Let me share a conversation I had with Danny, the owner and operator of three thriving businesses, to illustrate the pernicious effects of "have-tos."

Danny: I used to enjoy the challenge. Now, I just go through the day waiting for it to pass. I've lost my motivation. I'm tired and stressed all the time. I worry incessantly about everything. I'm just worn out.

Dr. G.: I bet you $100 that you've changed your attitude for the worse in the last year or so.

Danny: What do you mean?

Dr. G.: Let me take a flyer and you tell me if I'm wrong. I'll bet you that contrary to the time when you were still motivated, challenged, and vital, you have adopted a life-or-death attitude toward your work: "I *have to* succeed . . . I *have to* keep the customer . . . I *have to* make the money."

Danny: Right! It's even like that with the boat my wife and I bought. Since
          it's sitting on the lake, I think I have to go down and use it.
Dr. G.:   That's exactly right. That "have-to" attitude has a grip on you. What
          you are doing is starting with something you want to do or make
          happen (such as succeed at work, or enjoy the boat) and then, in
          your mind, you've converted it into a "have-to," a "must." You're
          making everything into an all-or-none, life-or-death crisis. Thinking
          like that would de-motivate and de-energize a horse.

Danny understood my message and worked to eliminate his life-or-death "have-to" thinking; he relaxed and gradually reclaimed his energy and vitality. You see, whenever people take something they desire and frame it in their mind as a "have-to," they tear down their vitality. For, if one believes it is absolutely necessary to have to produce or accomplish some desirable outcome, one inevitably feels pressure and stress; and, in failing to produce or accomplish what is thought to absolutely be necessary, one will consequently feel depressed and be emotionally destroyed. These emotional reactions certainly drain energy and siphon vitality.

The truth is that there are no absolute "have-tos" in the universe. While highly desirable, we do not have to succeed at our business, have the respect of any particular other, or reap the fruits of our labor. Nor do others have to behave in ways that we want. We do not even have to continue to live, though I presume we all would find that highly desirable.

The key to this intensifier is to live within the best of two philosophic worlds. The first is to deeply, even passionately desire what we value or want; this gives us enthusiasm and energy. The second is to never turn any desire into a necessity, a "have-to," for this inevitably brings emotional pain and becomes a drag on our vitality.

Cultivate a Sense of Humor

The essence of most all emotional disturbance is to take ourselves and life too seriously. Think about it: the beliefs that I have to do well, be liked, be treated well by others, and have things work out my way are deadly serious indeed. They inevitably lead to anxiety, anger, and/or depression.

What better way to relax, chill out, and enjoy the bumpy ride of life than to learn to laugh at ourselves and life's vagaries. There is perhaps no better example of this than the great American humorist Samuel Clemens (1835–1910), who, under the pen name Mark Twain, wrote the classic stories of *Huckleberry Finn*, *Tom Sawyer*, *Pudd'nhead Wilson*, and *The Notorious Jumping Frog of Calaveras County*. Clemens' sense of humor illuminated his everyday life as well. His oldest daughter Clara wrote, "Father was always ready to makes jokes at the breakfast table. I would say that my father was the only one at the table who found real joy in life so early in the morning, and of course he didn't find it, he created it" (Clemens, 1931, p. 3).

Samuel Clemens retained his sense of humor his whole life, believing it was the key to making life enjoyable and rich. He wrote, "Humor is the great thing, the saving thing, after all. The minute it crops up, all our hardnesses yield, all our irritations and resentments flit away, and a sunny spirit takes their place" (Twain, 1895, p. 61).

Be a Proactive Problem Solver

So often we end up in crisis because we don't handle our responsibilities in a timely manner. If you don't check the oil in your car, you will eventually blow the engine. If you don't exercise on a regular basis, your body will deteriorate. If you don't save your money over many years, you will have a difficult financial time in your elder years. If you don't identify and remedy problems in your business or career, you will find your profits jeopardized.

Reserving time in your monthly schedule to identify existing problems and anticipating future ones can benefit you in any number of ways. By handling these problems in a timely manner, you will keep yourself out of crisis, prevent these incompletions from nagging at you, and prevent stress. Equally as valuable, you can feel satisfied with your efforts and keep your vitality up.

AN ORGANIZATIONAL CASE STUDY

As critical as Robust Vitality is for individual greatness, so too is it necessary for organizational greatness as well. Though an organization's financial and physical assets are important, the human assets trump all. After all, people control these other assets.

The best example I have of an organization that actively promoted Robust Vitality is Vanco Beverage, the beer distributorship that hired me as a driver's helper in the summers both before and after my senior years in college. Along with my driver Walt, my job was to load up the truck with cases of Falls City, Budweiser, and Busch Bavarian beer first thing in the morning and then, throughout the day, to roll hand-trucks stacked with cases of beer into virtually every tavern, grocery store, and liquor store within the city limits of Evansville, Indiana. Once we stacked the cases in the establishment, we loaded up the cases of empty bottles to return to the warehouse.

This was not the most stimulating or challenging of jobs, but Earl Schmadel, the company owner, made sure the employees enjoyed their work. First of all, he opened a recreation room where employees could lounge after work for as long as they wanted. Available were card tables, a huge TV, and a tapped keg of beer, all to be used as late into the evening as wanted. There were only two rules: (1) if you emptied a keg, you had to roll another one in and tap it; (2) if you were the last one to leave at night, you had to turn off all the lights and lock up the warehouse.

The care and feeding of the vitality of his employees didn't stop there. Mr. Schmadel also hosted a fish fry in the warehouse the last Friday of each month, and took the entire employee body to a St. Louis Cardinals baseball game in the summer and a St. Louis Cardinals football game in the fall. He also treated everyone to steak dinners at a local restaurant twice a year. At all these functions, he provided huge bowls filled with jumbo shrimp and washtubs full of bottled beer covered in ice.

But, Earl Schmadel didn't limit his efforts to bucking up the vitality of his workforce with only social and sports events. In addition to those vitality-building perks, he also supported his employees in the following ways:

- He made sure that every one of his employees saw that their job had relevance to the overall success of the business.
- He purchased for his employees the type of health insurance that covered both physical illnesses and mental health issues, including drug and alcohol treatment.
- He arranged memberships at a local health club for any employee who wanted to join.
- He made available through Evansville College continuing education courses, seminars, and workshops that had relevance to job performance, career advancement, and emotional and interpersonal well-being.
- He offered employees the opportunity to attend seminars on such topics as smoking cessation, nutrition, conflict resolution, effective communication, anger release, and teamwork.

Earl Schmadel was a man ahead of his time. He provided a role model for those in leadership roles who would be wise to actively promote Robust Vitality in their workforce. He knew that exhausted, dull, stressed, and interpersonally conflicted work crew will be anything but productive.

A FINAL WORD

Robust Vitality is only one of the traits to bring Unrelenting Drive, Dedication, and Determination to producing the greatness in life you want. But, it may be the foundation. For, without physical, mental, and emotional vitality, it will be very difficult for anyone to sustain the use of the other traits.

I strongly urge you to follow through on your Robust Vitality action plan. If you've developed a cogent, reasonable plan, you will not only experience a leap in your vitality, but also a jump in your enjoyment of life.

REFERENCES AND SUGGESTED READING

Cashman, K. (1998). *Leadership from the inside out.* Provo, UT: Executive Excellence Publishing.

Clemens, C. (1931). *My father Mark Twain.* New York & London: Harper Brothers Publications.

Covey, S. R. (1989). *The 7 habits of highly effective people.* New York: Simon & Schuster.

Niebuhr, R. (1987). *The essential Reinhold Niebuhr: Selected essays.* New Haven, CT: Yale University Press.

Rivers, M. and DeMarco, M. (2003). *Aren't no sense worryin: The wisdom of Mick "the Quick" Rivers.* Champaign, IL: Sports Publishing LLC.

Sherwood, B. (2009). *The survivors club.* New York: Grand Central Publishing.

Thoreau, H. D. (n.d.). Available at: www.forbes.com/quotes/3974 (accessed November 16, 2016).

Twain, M. (1895). "What Paul Bourget thinks of us." *The North American Review,* 160(458), 48–63.

Wygal, W. C. (1940). *We plan our own workshop services: Business girls practice the act and art of group worship.* New York: The Women's Press.

CHAPTER 8

Harmony at Home[1]

A happy home life – the foundation for laser-like focus, zest, and powerful effort

Let no one ever come to you without leaving better and happier.
Mother Teresa

Take a minute to think about how your day goes when things are tense at home. If like me, your mood is contaminated with frustration, irritation, and even hurt. You don't feel as energetic and motivated as you normally do. You find it difficult to stay focused on and involved in the task at hand. Not exactly a formula for extraordinary performance and results, is it?

In contrast, when your home front is happy and harmonious, don't you feel centered and content? Don't you find that you have a spring in your step and that your thoughts are clear and focused? Isn't it true that you can then direct all your energy toward securing coveted goals?

It doesn't take a genius to know this to be true for most people. Your husband, wife, or significant other can be a strong wind at your back on sunny days, and a safe haven in stormy weather. On the other hand, he or she can be a burden that weighs you down, a contaminant that poisons your ability to put out your full and best effort.

The sad fact, though, is that creating and maintaining an intimate relationship, one that aids and abets Unrelenting Drive, Dedication, and Determination, is difficult. One of my favorite quotes comes from the noted psychiatrist, Lawrence Kubie. Way back in 1956, he stated, "Men and women are infinitely ingenious in their ability to find new ways of being unhappy together, so that even with unlimited space it would be impossible to illustrate every variety of marital misery" (Kubie, 1956).

How true, especially when one takes a look at all the challenges mated life throws our way. These include:

- the fact that we inevitably mate with a fallible human being – a man or woman who will, at least on occasion, provide us with frustrations, annoyances, and deprivations;

- the inevitable loss of some degree of privacy, variety, novelty, time, and energy;
- the number of issues about which two people can differ and that can even lead to conflict, such as finances, childrearing, in-laws, sex, and religion, among many others things;
- the unlikelihood that any two people will be totally compatible across the breadth of all the non-tangible issues they must negotiate, including power, control, nurturance, intimacy, trust, fidelity, and loyalty;
- the fact that very few people possess all the skills necessary to successfully manage a relationship (e.g., communication, fair fighting, parenting), leading inevitably to two people sometimes handling adversity poorly.

This litany of relationship landmines can be challenging for any two people. But these do not exhaust the list. Added to these are the romantic myths that people often harbor about their primary relationship, some of which can prove to be deadly if acted upon. Chief among them is the myth that love conquers all – that love, once bloomed, will unconditionally endure, needing neither watering nor pruning.

A few years ago, I provided leadership training to the management team of a luxury hotel in the Caribbean. Lunching one day with its director of wedding services, I asked her what was the biggest insight she took away after assisting hundreds of couples tie the knot. She answered, "Most couples spend more time planning their wedding than they do their marriage."

What an observation – one I observe daily in my clinical psychology office. I have seen very few couples who have created a blueprint to insure that their relationship stays happy and harmonious. That is why I devote the rest of this chapter to laying out what I have learned to be the root source of Harmony at Home. If two people will – on purpose – master these character traits, they will not only increase their life's satisfaction, but they will also secure the peace-of-mind at home that lends itself to full-out, focused productivity elsewhere in their lives.

THE ROOT SOURCE OF HARMONY AT HOME

Let me take you back to the metaphor of a tree that I originally introduced in Chapter 1 (see Figure 8.1). Just as a tree cannot produce its fruit unless it is solid at its trunk and healthy at its roots, so too will a person be unable to produce the fruit of great results unless he or she is solid at his or her trunk (skillful) and especially healthy at his or her roots (of sound character).

To generate the kind of Harmony at Home that energizes a person to produce great results, a person will need to act skillfully to make this happen; for

Results

Greatness
(However One
Defines It)

Means

Skillfulness

Source

Character

FIGURE 8.1   The Tree of Extraordinary Relationships

example, he or she will need to act with affection and interest toward his or her partner, be willing to make compromises when in disagreement, and so on. But there are many people who have mastered the skills, yet still fail to achieve harmony with their significant other. What I have observed is that these people fail because they are weak at their roots – that is, they are deficient or dysfunctional in the necessary character traits that spawn the full use of the skills they may indeed have.

I now share three relationship character traits that power the effective use of all relationship skills. They are: Premeditated Acceptance and Forgiveness; Relentless and Intelligent Giving; and 100% Relationship Responsibility (Figure 8.2). I have never seen two people who possess these traits fail in their primary relationship, thereby creating the Harmony at Home that frees them to produce great results outside the home.

Harmony at Home Trait 1: Premeditated Acceptance and Forgiveness

Here is an often-ignored relationship reality: we never mate with a saint or an angel. Being a fallible, imperfect person, our partner will at times treat us poorly. He or she will bring faults, idiosyncrasies, and sometimes even emotional problems to us. We can bank on him or her, at times, committing (1) sins of commission (doing what we don't want), and (2) sins of omission (not doing what we do want).

The truth is that your partner, my partner, and everyone else's partner will occasionally act unreasonably, irritably, and even rudely. At other times, he or

**Premeditated Acceptance
and Forgiveness**

**Harmony
at
Home**

**Relentless and
Intelligent Giving**

**100% Relationship
Responsibility**

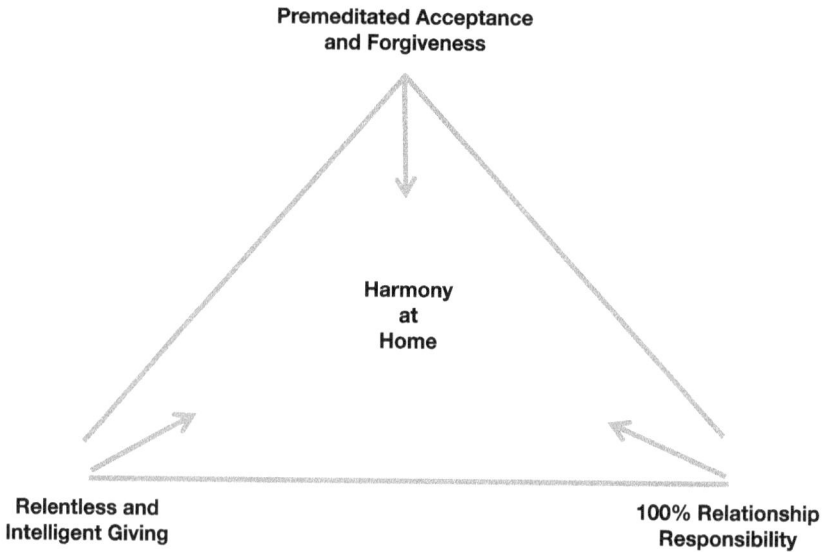

FIGURE 8.2   Relationship Character Traits

she will ignore us, withhold affection, or fail to follow through on promises. The issue is not whether this will happen, but when.

The challenge we all face when confronted with our beloved's fallibility is how to respond. Wise people, those who rarely show up in my clinical office, deal gracefully with these moments. For starters, they hold realistic expectations, accepting the fact that their partner will not always act saintly. Then, when their mate misbehaves, they don't overreact emotionally and either gracefully let it slide or calmly sit down and talk it out.

The people whom I see in my office, however, often don't respond so wisely. They react with the emotional contaminants of hurt and anger. Why do I call these feelings "contaminants"? Because they contaminate a person's ability to communicate effectively, cooperate in productive problem solving, and act in ways that do not prompt reciprocal emotional contamination in the partner. Moreover, their hurt and anger often spills over into the rest of their lives, impairing their productivity throughout the day.

I could describe hundreds of couples who have fallen into this hurt and anger trap. Take the case of Bill and Nancy. Nancy's grievous sin of omission, according to Bill, was what he called her sexual frigidity, desiring sex a mere once a week. For him, four times a week was more like it.

Unfortunately, Bill held rather unrealistic expectations of Nancy, demanding that she be wired exactly as he wanted, at least with regard to sex. In his mind, Nancy's not desiring sex more often was a personal rejection of him. The more he thought this way, the more hurt and angry he felt.

Not to be outdone, Nancy in turn reacted angrily back toward Bill. Also ignoring the fact that Bill too was a fallible human being who would inevitably commit sins of commission, she stated, "How dare he! He's reduced our marriage to sex, treating me as if I were a piece of meat." As you can imagine, as Nancy's anger went north, her libido went further south. And, predictably, in response to her further diminished libido, Bill's anger predictably increased.

With their negative feelings running rampant, Bill and Nancy found it more and more difficult to feel close, express tenderness, and sustain their bond. To the contrary, they reported that their sour mood pretty much spoiled the rest of their day, along with their focus and their drive.

Like so many of my couple clients, both Bill and Nancy needed to master Premeditated Acceptance and Forgiveness. It boiled down to adopting the following three relationship character principles.

Take Nothing Personally

Personalization means that, when your significant other acts in some contrary way toward you, you assume that it either reflects that he or she doesn't care or that he or she did it personally out of disrespect. This fallacy proved to be the case with Bill and Nancy.

- When asked what it meant to him that Nancy desired sex only once a week, Bill said, "She doesn't find me attractive or really love me."
- When Nancy was asked the same question about Bill's frustration and anger, she responded, "He must not respect me as a person."

Notice that both Bill and Nancy assumed that the other's behavior came from an uncaring, malevolent place and was thus an act of hostility purposely acted against them. It's conceivable that that may be true in a few cases, but this is rarely so. The truth is that one's partner disappoints, frustrates, or acts badly because he or she is a fallible human being, one who's put together psychologically in his or her unique way, thereby acting in the obnoxious manner he or she on occasion does. It's not personal.

Imagine if Bill and Nancy had processed their partner's respective sin in a non-personal way. Think of the emotional contamination they would have prevented if they thought along the following lines:

- Bill: "I'm not crazy about the fact that Nancy is sexually wired the way she is. It's frustrating for me because I find her so attractive. But it's just the way she is. It's not about or against me."
- Nancy: "Bill sure is acting childish about all this. I don't like it, but it's not because he doesn't respect me. It's just the way he responds to his frustration and hurt."

Don't Expect Perfection

Expecting perfection is most often betrayed by the use of the words "should", "ought," or "must," as in, "She should be more responsive," or, "He shouldn't act like that." Forgetting that we are mated with an imperfect human being who must, at least on occasion, act badly, we perfectionistically assume that our partner will never act in a contrary way.

Both Bill and Nancy fell into the trap of expecting perfection from each other. Listen to the interchange I had with Bill:

> Dr. G.: Bill, when you think about Nancy not being as sexually interested as you want her to be, what do you tell yourself?
>
> Bill: Well, I don't like it.
>
> Dr. G.: But, Bill, if you just thought, "I don't like it, but that's just Nancy," you'd only feel frustrated or disappointed, not angry. I'm hearing a "should." What is it? Finish this sentence: "I don't like it that Nancy isn't more sexually interested, and she ..."
>
> Bill: She should be!
>
> Dr. G.: That's right! You're saying to yourself, "My fallible, imperfect wife, Nancy, should perfectly be the way I want her to be, at least sexually.'
>
> Bill: I guess you're right. I am thinking that way.
>
> Dr. G.: And that kind of thinking is what gets you mad. For, if there is some law of nature that commands Nancy to be exactly, perfectly, the way you want her to be sexually, and she is breaking that law, then I guess anger is justified. But, one, she is not perfect to begin with, and, two, there is no such law. Right?
>
> Bill: But, I know she's not perfect. Nobody is.
>
> Dr. G.: But Bill, if you indeed operated on the premise that Nancy is a fallible person, who will inevitably let you down, would you have reacted with so much hurt and anger?
>
> Bill: I guess not.

While Nancy listened to this exchange, I could see that she was gratified by Bill's chastened look. Not to let her off the hook, I said to her, "Now, Nancy, isn't the same thing true for you? Let's assume that Bill is incorrect in responding as he does. Like Bill, aren't you also secretly demanding that he be perfect, never treating you unfairly?" Sheepishly, she acknowledged I was correct, saying, "I guess you're right on!"

So, both Bill and Nancy, by their demand for perfection from their partner, set themselves up for the relationship disturbance of hurt and anger. The choice a couple makes between these two expectations at B – perfection or imperfection – forms the context in which their relationship plays out. For, if you consciously or unconsciously expect your partner to be perfect, you will not only be regularly disappointed and let down, but frequently offended, hurt, and angry as well.

Again, imagine if both Bill and Nancy had processed each other's dislikable behavior in a more realistic manner, not liking but understanding that he or she can't be perfect. It would sound something like the following and, though maybe experiencing some frustration, neither would carry hurt or anger inside them.

> I sure wish my partner would act more to my liking. But, he/she's human and can neither be perfect nor always be my all and everything. Where do I get off expecting him/her to be an angel? Forgive and forget.

Never Damn

Damning our partner drives the final nail into the hurt and anger coffin. It starts with a rational desire for our partner to act differently, as in, "I don't like what you're doing, I wish you'd stop that." But, it then quickly evolves into a total damnation of the person, as per, "You shouldn't do this, you blankety-blank."

Let's once more visit Bill and Nancy. Notice how they each damned the other with a negative label or name-call.

Bill: She should be more interested in sex than she is. She's just a cold, frigid person.

Nancy: All he seems to think about is sex. He should just get off it and appreciate me for who I am. What a fool he is.

But let's look at the truth. Although your partner will indeed have faults and act badly, he or she is not a totally bad person or any other pejorative global term, such as a frigid person or a fool. Despite the traits or behaviors you dislike in your partner, he or she has many other traits and behaviors, a good many of which are positive. He or she is not just this one thing that you dislike.

Once again, let's use Bill to pull it all together. Imagine him applying the following way of thinking to the rest of his days with Nancy. This would represent the essence of Premeditated Acceptance and Forgiveness, as well as the end of his hurt and anger.

> I sure wish Nancy were more sexually minded, but her sexual style is simply a reflection of the way she's wired. It's not about me at all. In fact, when I think about it, she should be exactly as she is – good, bad, or indifferent. There's no law that commands her to magically be exactly the way I want. Besides, she is a warm, loving woman in virtually every way imaginable.

There's no sense in me being emotionally upset about it on top of being sexually frustrated.

One final word before I take you to the Premeditated Acceptance and Forgiveness Workshop. While I am all for relationship harmony and happiness for its own sake, don't forget that Harmony at Home is one of the root sources of producing extraordinary performance and results. Being content and peaceful in one's primary relationship lends itself to productivity outside the home.

The Premeditated Acceptance and Forgiveness Workshop

This workshop begins the process of creating and sustaining Harmony at Home. It consists of identifying your hurt- and anger-producing beliefs, then showing yourself how incorrect they are, and lastly replacing them with more realistic, accepting, and forgiving ones.

Take note, though, that deeply endorsing and strongly adopting these mindsets will take practice. Whether working on your own or under the guidance of a professional clinician, consultant, or coach, be prepared to repeat the steps in this workshop many times. But, I guarantee you that your results will be well worth the effort.

Step One: Develop Mindfulness

Premeditated Acceptance and Forgiveness starts with mindfulness. Being aware of your hurt and anger pattern provides you with the opportunity to rid yourself of them. Reflect on your relationship with your significant other. What does he or she do to which you react with hurt and anger? Then note how you typically behave once emotionally contaminated. Lastly, describe the outcome of your reactions. Do they help or hinder Harmony at Home? Improve or worsen the situation? The relationship? After doing this, note a few ways you could behave differently at these times so as not to escalate the situation or to do harm to your relationship.

What Happens	My Reaction	The Outcome
1. _____	_____	_____
_____	_____	_____
2. _____	_____	_____
_____	_____	_____
3. _____	_____	_____
_____	_____	_____

Some positive changes in how I react might be: _____

_____

_____

_____

_____

Step Two: Take Responsibility

Now you have a clear picture of your hurt and anger pattern. Step Two asks you to take responsibility for your emotional and behavioral reactions. Remember that you are the one who creates the way you react by the meaning you make of what your partner does. It is you taking it personally, demanding perfection, and/or damning him or her. To accept and forgive your partner, even before he or she misbehaves, you need to take full responsibility for the fact that you yourself, not him or her, have upset yourself.

Note the difference between the following pair of statements that Bill could have made. The first blames Nancy for his hurt and anger. In the second, he takes full responsibility for how he acted.

1. "Nancy hurt my feelings by not wanting more sex."
2. "I caused myself to feel hurt and anger by interpreting Nancy's not wanting more sex as a personal rejection."

The benefits of your taking responsibility for your own hurt and anger are several. First, it has integrity, for you do indeed cause yourself to feel these ways. Second, by accepting responsibility, you can forgive your partner, relinquish your hurt and anger, and get on with the process of living in harmony. Third, and most profound, you can adopt the characterological mindsets of Premeditated Acceptance and Forgiveness as a way of relationship life.

Step Two, then, is where the rubber hits the road. Unless your partner magically transforms into a perfect saint or angel, never again treating you badly, you are doomed to a ton of relationship disharmony without taking responsibility for your reactions. So, reflect carefully and, if willing, sign the following responsibility pledge.

I, _____, take full responsibility for the anger and/or hurt I feel toward my partner, _____.
When he/she does _____,
_____, and _____,

I cause myself to feel these ways. I therefore commit to eliminate my hurt and anger, regardless of whether or not my partner alters his/her behavior.

Signed _____

Date   _____

Step Three: Identify Your Irrational Thinking

There is one – and only one – meaning to your hurt and anger. It is that you are causing yourself to experience these contaminating feelings by irrationally taking your partner's behavior personally, demanding that he or she be perfect, and damning him or her for imperfection. Step Three asks you to track down these self-talks each and every time you get upset with your mate. Once uncovered, you can dispel their validity in Step Four. Write below in complete sentence form how you state these thoughts to yourself. They are what you will need to eliminate in order to rid yourself of hurt and anger.

My Partner's Behavior	My Irrational Thinking
1. _____	1. _____
2. _____	2. _____
3. _____	3. _____

Step Four: Subject Your Beliefs to Skeptical Disputation

Step Four makes use of the power of skepticism. In this step, you hold each of your irrational beliefs up as a hypothesis, not a predetermined fact, and rigorously dispute its validity until you convince yourself that it is incorrect.

By way of caution, I emphasize that changing the way you think is not easy. You must repeatedly and energetically show yourself the irrationality of these thoughts in order to eliminate them from your mind. To prep you for this disputation to follow, I offer you three cheat sheets.

Taking It Personally Cheat Sheet

- Your partner does not lay awake at night gleefully thinking of ways to hurt you, deny you, or put you down.

- Your partner acts badly because of the way he or she is psychologically put together, not to get under your skin.
- Even when angry at you, your partner acts spitefully because of the habitual way he or she has learned to handle adversity.

Demanding Perfection Cheat Sheet

- Your partner is not perfect. Being imperfect, he or she will periodically do things you don't like, as well as not do things you do like. This is a reality, so expect it.
- No matter how annoying or frustrating it may be, your partner must or should be exactly as he or she is. After all, your partner spent a lifetime evolving into his or her unique personality, no matter how flawed this may be or how much you wish certain of his or her traits, foibles, or weaknesses were different.
- While you have every right to dislike what your partner does, and even to assertively (but not angrily) attempt to get him or her to change, it never follows that, because you don't like it, he or she shouldn't act in the ways you dislike. After all, you don't as yet run the universe or own this person.

Damnation Cheat Sheet

- Although your partner will indeed have faults and act badly, he or she is not a totally bad person or any other pejorative, global term (e.g., a frigid person, a fool).
- While you may judge what he or she does, it is never appropriate to judge or damn your partner as a whole person.
- Despite the traits or behaviors you dislike in your partner, he or she has many other traits and behaviors, a good many of which are positive. He or she is not just this one thing you dislike.

Now let's get to work. In Step Three, you identified the irrational thinking that causes you to feel hurt and anger toward your partner. Using the power of skepticism, aggressively dispute each of your hurt- and anger-producing beliefs until you've convinced yourself that they are not true. Don't forget to refer to your cheat sheets to help you.

1. **My partner's difficult behavior:** _____

_____

_____

_____

My hurt-/anger-producing belief: _____

_____

_____

_____

Why this belief is untrue and invalid: _____

_____

_____

_____

2. My partner's difficult behavior: _____

_____

_____

_____

My hurt-/anger-producing belief: _____

_____

_____

_____

Why this belief is untrue and invalid: _____

_____

_____

_____

3. My partner's difficult behavior: _____

_____

_____

_____

My hurt-/anger-producing belief: _____

_____

_____

_____

Why this belief is untrue and invalid: _____

_____

_____

_____

Step Five: Adopting Premeditated Acceptance and Forgiveness

Now that you've shown yourself how absurd the beliefs that spawn your hurt and anger are, you're now poised to indoctrinate yourself with ones that build Premeditated Acceptance and Forgiveness and that lead you to respond accordingly when your partner acts in contrary ways. This statement could specifically reference the behaviors you find offensive or it could be a more generic one that could be applied to all future offensives.

Here is the rational thought Bill created specifically with regard to Nancy and sex. Notice that, if he genuinely endorsed it, it would be impossible for him to make himself angry and hurt.

> I sure wish Nancy were more sexually minded, but her sexual style is simply a reflection of the way she is wired. It's not about me at all. In fact, she should be exactly as she is, particularly because there's no law that commands her to be the way I want. There is no sense in me being emotionally upset about it on top of being sexually frustrated.

Now, below, create your own rational, anti-hurt/-anger belief. Do so for the specific things about which you cause yourself to feel hurt and anger and a more general one that could be applied to any and all instances of dislikable behavior by your significant other going forward.

Specific Premeditated Acceptance and Forgiveness belief: _____

_____

_____

_____

General Premeditated Acceptance and Forgiveness belief: _____

_____

_____

_____

Great job on this workshop. The more you practice your new Premeditated Acceptance and Forgiveness beliefs, the more automatic they will become and the less hurt and angry you will feel. Then you will not only reap the benefits of a happy, harmonious home life, but you will also be free of the emotional contaminants that block energy and focused on creating great results.

Harmony at Home Trait 2: Relentless and Intelligent Giving

In my book *The Couples Therapy Companion* (2015), I shared the following joke:

> A husband and wife seek out a counselor after 45 years of marriage. The counselor asks them what's the problem. The wife goes into a tirade, listing every problem they have ever had in all the 45 years they've been married. She goes on and on.
>
> Finally, the counselor gets up, embraces the woman, and kisses her passionately. The woman sits stupefied.
>
> The counselor turns to the husband and says, "That is what your wife needs, at least three times a week. Can you do that?"
>
> The husband thinks for a moment and replies, "Well, I can get her here Mondays and Wednesdays, but on Fridays I play golf."

The point to this joke is that the quality of your relationship is in direct proportion to the amount of yourself and your affection you give to your partner. To say it another way, a relationship will only prosper to the extent that a person relentlessly and intelligently makes his or her partner feel significant and loved.

- How so relentlessly? By giving love and affection to your partner each and every day. This will predictably invigorate your partner's appreciation for and satisfaction with you, likely motivating him or her to give love and affection back to you.
- How so intelligently? By giving love and affection in exactly the ways your partner most desires. You see, not everybody feels loved by the same expressions. So, you need to not only be relentless in your giving, but you must do so intelligently as well.

The husband in this joke was neither relentless nor intelligent. He failed to give his wife the attention and affection she so desperately wanted. Predictably, she became increasingly annoyed, in turn making any possibility for Harmony at Home impossible.

Let me illustrate this with a real-life case example. When I first met Peter and Kathy, they stated that their marital disharmony stemmed from poor communication. In talking with them, I found that poor communication was only the surface issue. Below the surface, both Peter and Kathy felt quite unloved by and rather insignificant to the other.

Let's drop in on an interchange I had with Peter during the early part of their first marital counseling session:

Dr. G.:	Peter, I can hear how frustrated you are with Kathy about sex and money. But, I get the distinct feeling that there is something more on your mind – perhaps something missing for you in your marriage about which you're frustrated, discouraged, or disillusioned. Am I right? What is it?
Peter:	(After a long pause and a deep sigh) Doc, I don't feel very special, like I'm just a piece of furniture to her.
Dr. G.:	Well, how so?
Peter:	I used to feel number one in her life, that she really adored me. Now I feel I'm just about last on her list – behind her work, the kids, her exercise, her friends, just about everything.
Dr. G.:	What did she use to do that made you feel so special? Something, maybe, that she has stopped doing?
Peter:	Lots of things. When I came home, she'd greet me at the door, take a few minutes to ask about my day, tell me about hers. She'd spend time with me in the evenings. She'd ride along with me in the cart while I played golf. Lots of things like that.
Dr. G.:	And this made you feel special?
Peter:	Absolutely.
Dr. G.:	And now?
Peter:	I just feel so alone.
Dr. G.:	How does this affect your motivation to show your love to Kathy?
Peter:	It pretty much kills it.

While talking to Peter I could see Kathy squirming. Not wanting this to become an indictment of her, I quickly turned to her:

Dr. G.:	I bet my bottom dollar, Kathy, that you feel pretty much the same way as Peter, but in reverse.
Kathy:	You bet! Peter is very self-focused. By his own admission, he's not really cut out for marriage.

Dr. G.:	Can you explain what you mean?
Kathy:	He doesn't really show much affection toward me or interest in what's important to me – my work, my friends, my passions. Unless it's focused on him, there's just nothing.
Dr. G.:	So it's very important to you for Peter to demonstrate that he cares about you and at the very least to show some interest in what is going on in your life?
Kathy:	Very much so.
Dr. G.:	Did he show you affection and interest when you were first together?
Kathy:	More so than now.
Dr. G.:	How did he do that?
Kathy:	He gave me hugs, held my hand, complimented me. He asked about things in my life. He listened when I shared.
Dr. G.:	How did it make you feel?
Kathy:	Very special. It's what I always wanted from a man.
Dr. G.:	And how do you now react when you don't get these affirmations?
Kathy:	I climb further into my own life. Why wouldn't I? That's where I get all my strokes.

From these exchanges, I felt confident that I had gotten to the core of Peter and Kathy's marital disharmony. They both failed the Relentless and Intelligent Giving character principle. They each would have to commit to making each other feel like number one once again to salvage their marriage.

Fortunately, they both did. I'll never forget their last session. Peter took my hand and said, "Thank you, Doc, we've got our marriage back."

So, before getting to the Relentless and Intelligent Giving workshop, here are four takeaways for sustaining Harmony at Home:

1. Everyone wants to feel significant to and loved by another person. It is not taught to us; it's built into our DNA.

2. But, there's a complication. While everyone wants to feel significant and loved, not everyone feels significant and loved in the same way. Some feel loved through physical actions, others through verbal expressions, and still others through quality time. So, it's not enough to simply show love and affection to your partner. You must show it in the exact ways that matter most to your partner.

3. If you meet Mr. or Ms. Right, you two will only sustain your love for each other if you both continue to give each other exactly what you each want and need to feel loved and significant. If you two fail at this, your love for each other will eventually dissipate and die. This is not romantic, but it's absolutely true.

4. Here is the bottom line. If you are wise, you and your partner will take the time to figure out exactly what you need to feel loved by and

significant to each other. This represents, in effect, your relationship job description. Then, if smart, you two will mindfully, purposefully, and consistently act to do your job. By relentlessly and intelligently making each other feel loved and significant in exactly the ways that matter most to each of you, you will give yourselves the best chance to keep your harmony and happiness at home bright and shiny.

The Relentless and Intelligent Giving Workshop

Armed with these insights, you are now primed to tackle the Relentless and Intelligent Giving workshop. It is modeled on Dr. Paul Hauck's (1994) simple three-step process of first understanding each other's wants and needs, then freeing yourselves to deliver the goods, and finally acting.

It is best if you and your partner tackle this workshop together. But don't despair if your partner declines to participate. By you taking it on your own shoulders to relentlessly and intelligently give to your partner, there is a good chance your partner will eventually enroll in the process. After all, a happy spouse – one who feels significant to and loved by you – will predictably be motivated to also give back to you.

Step One: Assure Understanding

The first step to Relentless and Intelligent Giving is to understand exactly what each of you needs from the other to feel significant and loved. This means that both of you must discover what you yourself value and then clearly communicate it to the other.

First, focus on yourself. What is it that you want and need from your partner in order to feel significant and loved? Following the thinking of Gary Chapman in his excellent book *The Five Love Languages* (1995), you might want to think along the lines of these five categories: (1) words of love, appreciation, and affection; (2) quality time; (3) receiving gifts; (4) acts of help and service; (5) physical expressions. Pick your top two and define them behaviorally so your partner will know exactly what he or she needs to do.

My Top Two	Behavioral Expressions
1. _____	_____
_____	_____
2. _____	_____
_____	_____

Once you are clear about what you want and need from your partner, you must communicate it so that he or she clearly understands. What might you say to your partner to help him or her become aware of your wants and needs? Remember that your job is to communicate about you, not about your partner. This communication, in other words, is designed to raise his or her awareness of you, not to critique your partner's past behavior.

_____

_____

_____

_____

Now focus on your partner. What is it that your partner wants and needs from you in order to feel loved and significant? You will need this information so that you can purposely do the job for which you were hired. You need to listen without judgment so you can fully absorb what he or she has to say. If your partner is not participating, go directly to him or her and ask. Regardless, make sure to translate his or her top two into observable behavioral strategies on your part.

	His/Her Top Two	**Behavioral Expressions**
1.	_____	_____
	_____	_____
2.	_____	_____
	_____	_____

Step Two: Be Able

Without this deep understanding, you two will be flying by the seat of your pants. The success of your relationship will be a wish and a prayer. All you can do is hope for the best.

But, I offer a word of caution. While awareness is necessary, it is not sufficient. You must also be *able* to relentlessly and intelligently give exactly what your partner needs from you in order for him or her to feel loved and cherished. So, the questions you are now to answer are:

1. Am I able to relentlessly and intelligently give to my partner what he/she wants and needs from me?
2. Is my partner able to relentlessly and intelligently give to me what I want and need from him or her?

If the answers to both of these questions are "Yes," then go right to Step Three. But, if the answers to either of these questions is "No," then there is some work to be done. Remember: the quality of your relationship depends on both of you being able to deliver the goods.

Now, it's time for you and your partner to identify what may block you from relentlessly and intelligently giving to your partner exactly what he or she needs to feel wonderfully significant to and loved by you. Be aware that it is not enough to know what your blocks are: you have to be free yourself to give to your partner what he or she needs from you. Your relationship absolutely depends on this.

First, about you. From the list below, what are the things that block your ability to relentlessly and intelligently give to your partner? Also identify what triggers these – that is, the things in your life and/or what your partner does or does not do that prompt these. Most important, what could you do – on purpose – to interrupt and eliminate these patterns?

My Blocking Patterns	Triggers
Emotional upsets	_____
	_____
	_____
Tired and stressed	_____
	_____
	_____
Distractions	_____
	_____
	_____
Laziness/taking for granted	_____
	_____
	_____
Narcissism	_____
	_____
	_____
Other	_____
	_____
	_____

What I will do to interrupt these patterns so as to relentlessly and intelligently give to my partner: _____

_____

_____

_____

_____

Now, focus on your partner. What are some of the things that block your partner from being a relentless and intelligent giver to you? What do you do that may trigger him or her into this pattern? Lastly, what will you do to help eliminate these triggers? Take this on from the perspective of 100% Relationship Responsibility (to follow).

Partner's Blocking Patterns	Triggers I Provide
Emotional upsets	_____ _____ _____
Tired and stressed	_____ _____ _____
Distractions	_____ _____ _____
Laziness/taking for granted	_____ _____ _____
Narcissism	_____ _____ _____
Other	_____ _____ _____

What I will do to interrupt what I do to make it difficult for my partner to relentlessly and intelligently give to me: _____

_____

_____

_____

_____

Step Three: Act

It is important to realize that all the understanding and ability in the world is useless without action. The truth is that the only thing that produces a desired result is doing what is necessary to produce that result. Nothing will substitute for action.

For example, let's say you wanted your house painted. Understanding that your house needs painting won't get it done. Developing a plan to paint it won't get it painted. Hoping and praying for it to be painted will not do the job. Becoming a master painter will not do the trick. As simple as it sounds, the only way to get your house painted is to paint it.

The same is true with regard to the success of your relationship. To create the relationship of your dreams, you must act – relentlessly and intelligently – to make it so. So, once you understand what you need to do and see to it that you are indeed able to do it, you must act. The $64,000 questions, the ones that will make or break your relationship, are:

1. Will I commit to act in the exact ways so as to relentlessly and intelligently make my partner feel deeply important to and absolutely loved by me?
2. Will I act – day after day, week after week, month after month – to give my partner exactly what he or she wants and needs from me to feel significant and loved?

Referring to what you have learned about your partner in Step One, create your Relentless and Intelligent Giving action plan. Exactly what will you do to make your partner feel supremely significant to and loved by you? Where and when will you do it? How often? Do not leave this to chance. Instead, plan it, and do it on purpose!

What	Where & When	How Often
_____	_____	_____
_____	_____	_____
_____	_____	_____
_____	_____	_____
_____	_____	_____

With regard to your partner, remember that you cannot change him or her. You can only change your own behavior toward your partner. Taking the actions you listed earlier can help to influence him or her to do likewise toward you.

Similarly, rewarding your partner when he or she acts to make you feel significant and loved will predictably encourage him or her to do more of the same. So, when your partner acts lovingly toward you, what positive, appreciative things will you do in response?

What He/She Does	My Rewarding Response
_____	_____
_____	_____
_____	_____
_____	_____
_____	_____
_____	_____
_____	_____
_____	_____

Great job on this workshop. You now have a solid plan to make your relationship happy and harmonious. Remember, though, that you must follow through, not just today and tomorrow while this is fresh in your mind, but mindfully, purposely, and endlessly into the future. This takes us to the third and final Harmony at Home character trait, 100% Relationship Responsibility.

Harmony at Home Trait 3: 100% Relationship Responsibility

Let's look at a couple who deteriorated to the brink of disaster. Jerry and Bridgett at one time cared deeply for one another, but they had grown so distant that their relationship was almost non-existent. To make matters worse, neither of them had the vaguest clue what happened or why.

In a nutshell, Bridgett, not feeling loved or cherished by Jerry, turned to her two sisters for her emotional connection and spent most all her energy at home with her children. Jerry, feeling insignificant to Bridgett, reacted with sullen withdrawal. Both felt frustrated and lonely, living more as roommates, not spouses.

Notice the vicious circle. The more Bridgett withdrew from Jerry, the more Jerry withdrew from Bridgett. This prompted Bridgett to further withdraw from Jerry, in turn inviting Jerry to withdraw even further from her. And on it went, round and round, each feeling victimized by the other, and each feeling justified in their own withdrawal. By the time I met them, this pattern has persisted for over two years.

It is important to understand that both Jerry and Bridgett had fallen into a victim mentality, holding their partner responsible for causing their marital problems. So long as they each felt victimized, neither of them was willing to take the initiative to break the vicious circle in which they had become mired. So, I started the change process by asking them three questions.

- Question 1:   When do you think your problems began?
  Answer: Neither of them could remember.
- Question 2:   Who do you think first started your problem?
  Answer: Neither of them could remember.
- Question 3:   Who do you think is responsible for fixing the problem?
  Answer: They each said the other.

My initial goal was to convince Jerry and Bridgett to each take 100% responsibility for overcoming their problems and making their relationship once again thrive. Meeting separately, I asked each of them to rate on a scale from 1 to 10 how loved they felt by their partner. Both said a "2." To raise their consciousness to the roles they each played in their marital problems, I then asked them to rate, again on scale from 1 to 10, how loved they thought their partner felt. Interestingly, they each again responded again with a "2."

Having established a beachhead, I then gave both Jerry and Bridgett what I call "the speech." It was an attempt to get them each to individually take the initiative to reverse their marital-defeating patterns. Here is what I said to Bridgett:

Bridgett, I know how hurt and angry you are. But, I want you to know that Jerry deeply loves you. Deep down, he really craves to feel significant to and loved by you. His pulling away is a desperate attempt to avoid pain.

I know you feel very abandoned and hurt too, thinking Jerry holds all the cards. But, if you will only realize how deeply Jerry wants you to love him, you can save the day. How? By simply feeding him the significance and love he so much wants from you. If he begins to once again believe that you love him, he'll then knock himself out to make you feel significant and loved in return.

So, Bridgett, what I'm strongly urging you to do is to make a commitment – a 100%, no-holds-barred commitment – to make Jerry feel so special and loved that he'll appreciate you till his dying day. Now, I'll be here to coach you along the way, but it has to start with your commitment. What do you say? Will you sign on?

In my experience, significant, positive change can happen even when only one of the two people in a relationship follows this advice. Why? Because when one person takes 100% responsibility to display love, the other most often follows suit. Thankfully, both Jerry and Bridgett stepped up to the plate. And, as predicted, they succeeded beyond my wildest hopes. The more loving Bridgett acted, the more gratified Jerry felt. Then, with his newfound appreciation for Bridgett, he acted more loving toward her than he had in years. This then motivated Bridgett to act even more lovingly to Jerry, and so on. The end result was a victorious rather than a vicious circle whereby the good deeds of the one served to stimulate the good deeds of the other.

The truth is that in every couple there are two halves. One half is you, and the other half is your partner. Of these two halves, you are 100% responsible for your half. To say it another way, you are completely responsible for your half, while your partner is 0% responsible for how you choose to act.

So, in your relationship you have two choices. First, you can take the 50/50% stance. That is, you take the posture that you are willing to contribute your 50% but only if your partner does his or her part. As with Jerry and Bridgett, this represents immature, "nanny-nanny boo-boo" thinking, as per: "Since you didn't show me love, I won't show you the love you want; if you change, then I will."

Second, a person can take the proactive stance. It goes like this: "I am 100% responsible for how I act, the choices I make, and the results I want to produce in my relationship. My relationship depends 100% on me, and I will do whatever is necessary to make it work, despite the lapses of my partner." This is a 100%, no-holds-barred commitment. It really only takes one, but imagine the power if both partners adopt this principle. This is the commitment both Jerry and Bridgett adopted in the course of their couple counseling.

Sear this into your mind. Following the principle of 100% Relationship Responsibility, remember and follow:

- Each partner will on occasion inevitably fail the other. This is an inescapable reality.
- If a person holds a reactive mindset, he or she will very likely become resentful and retaliate in some way by shutting down and/or lashing out when his or her partner doesn't live up to expectations. This betrays a 50/50% victim mentality and will most likely prompt this person to start a downward- spiraling, relationship-destroying vicious circle.
- The more two people operate on the principle of 100% Relationship Responsibility – that is, taking 100% responsibility for doing what is necessary to make the relationship work – the better are their chances of creating a loving, lasting relationship.

The 100% Relationship Responsibility Workshop

So, 100% Relationship Responsibility is the third Harmony at Home character trait. Along with Premeditated Acceptance and Forgiveness and Intelligent and Relentless Giving, this trait can almost guarantee a bright, shiny home life. This in turn opens the door for a person to devote all his or her focus, energy, and talent to creating cherished results.

This workshop, though simple and straightforward, is profound, requiring courage, grit, and maturity. You may tackle it by yourself or, better yet, under the guidance of your clinician, consultant, or coach.

Step One: Conduct Self-Assessment

Where do you stand with regard to 100% Relationship Responsibility in your relationship with your significant other? Are you a 100%er or are you a 50/50%er?

On the continuum below, first rate with your initials where you fall. Then, using your partner's initials, rate where you think he or she would put you. After doing that, describe the results for you, your partner, and your relationship with regard to Harmony at Home.

	50/50%				100%	
Strong	moderate	slight		Strong	moderate	slight
3	2	1	0	3	2	1

The results of my 100% Relationship Responsibility stance: _____

_____

_____

_____

_____

_____

Step Two: Adjust Your Attitude

Remember that without the right attitude, you will find it next to impossible to respond gracefully to your partner when he or she doesn't hold up his or her end of the bargain. So, adopting 100% Relationship Responsibility toward your partner is the next step in your workshop.

Below, state exactly which belief you will hold with regard to your responsibility to making your relationship filled with happiness and harmony. Write it powerfully, positively, and with commitment. Start the sentence with "I will . . ." Refer back to Jerry and Bridgett to refresh yourself if necessary.

My 100% Relationship Responsibility stance will be: _____

_____

_____

_____

Step Three: Develop Your Action Plan

As stated before, no results are ever produced without action – that is, doing what is necessary to bring about those results. With regard to 100% Relationship Responsibility, list three things that you will do, regardless of how your partner behaves, to bring happiness and harmony to your relationship. Make sure these actions are important and significant.

1. _____

_____

_____

2. _____

_____

_____

3. _____

_____

_____

INTENSIFIERS

Now that you've completed the three Harmony at Home workshops, here are three intensifiers that can magnify any couple's harmony and happiness. The first is cognitive, while the last two are behavioral. I suggest the two people in a relationship practice them on purpose until they become habitual.

Focus On Your Partner's Strengths

No matter the relationship, one's partner, being a fallible human being, will embody both positive and negative qualities. Which of these a person chooses to focus on will determine to a large extent his or her feelings toward that partner. If he or she dwells on the partner's negative qualities, he or she will likely be chronically annoyed, frustrated, and unhappy with this person. To the contrary, by focusing on his or her positive qualities, this person cannot help but feel more positive and loving.

To enhance Harmony at Home, make a list of the positive qualities of your partner. Note the physical attributes you like, those strengths of character and personality you admire, and the endearing mannerisms you find delightful. Start each day and end each night reviewing these.

Connect Often

Happy, harmonious couples connect several times each and every day. They take pains to exchange goodbyes when parting and affectionate greetings when re-joining. They reach out to each other by phone, e-mail, and/or text during the course of the day. They make it a point to spend extended quality time together at least once a week. I urge every person who reads this book to add these ingredients to your relationship routine. They are all easy to do and effective.

Frequently Express Affection and Appreciation

Research shows us that a dearth of validating messages, frequent criticisms, and negative body language are highly predictive of divorce. As one would imagine, the opposite is true of frequent expressions of affection and appreciation.

The implications are obvious. To produce and sustain a relationship that thrives, two people would be wise to purposely express their admiration to each other at least once a day. They want to do this to become so accustomed to it that it becomes automatic.

AN ORGANIZATIONAL CASE STUDY

I hope by now I've sufficiently made the point that disharmony at home can easily contaminate a person's energy, focus, and productivity elsewhere in life. As a clinician, far too many people for me to count have testified that life in general works much better for them once they've made their home life more happy and harmonious.

One of the more fascinating discoveries of my consulting practice has been that the character traits that aid romantic couples to thrive also apply to business relationships. Once I realized this, I found that my couple-counseling techniques worked equally well in the workplace. I think of the junior partner in a dental practice who, because of his short fuse and belligerent behavior, destroyed the goodwill and trust of virtually everyone in the office. No one wanted to work with him and several employees experienced such upset that they resorted to antidepressant medication. It took the senior partner's threat to dissolve the partnership to prompt him to consult with me. After several months of weekly meetings, I finally succeeded in indoctrinating him with the principle of Premeditated Acceptance and Forgiveness. Once he adopted and acted in accordance with it, he slowly but surely built trust and goodwill with his colleagues.

Then there was the conflict between the director and assistant director of a public works department in a medium-sized city neighboring the Commonwealth of Virginia. Jack, the director, operated the department as his private fiefdom, unilaterally making most all decisions, rarely consulting with anyone else, and treating the assistant director, Jerry, like his administrative assistant. For his part, Jerry became more and more angry, showing up late for meetings, ignoring many of Jack's directives, and barely maintaining a civil tone. Needless to say, the ill will between these two top leaders did not go unnoticed among the leadership team and had the effect of undercutting overall morale.

I needed to bring to bear all my skills when I sat down with these two powerful personalities. Thankfully, through guile and persistence, I was able to convince both of them of the ultimate devastation of their downward spiral and prevailed upon each of them to adopt the 100% Relationship Responsibility principle. For his part, Jack dedicated himself to practicing Relentless and Intelligent Giving, thereby treating Jerry with the respect he wanted and deserved. Jerry also stepped up to the plate, gradually accepting that Jack did not act as he did out of disrespect, accepting Jack's fallibility, and forgoing the damning of him as a "jerk." These two men never became best friends, but they learned to work together cooperatively, peacefully, and productively.

The last example I'll give is that of Kimberly, the office manager of a large, bustling family medical practice. Short of patience, she responded to anything less than perfect performance as intolerable, peppering the staff with memo after memo of criticism, barking at her direct reports, and in general making the workday unpleasant for those around her. It took the threat of being fired to motivate her to work with me. After much struggle, she came to see the drawbacks of her style, the illogic of her perfectionistic ways of thinking, and the benefits of a new approach to managing the office. Slowly but surely, she shed the criticism that her perfectionistic thinking spawned, became more accepting and forgiving of the fallible people she oversaw, and integrated acts of appreciation and praise into her communication.

The bottom line is this: the three character traits that comprise Harmony at Home are universal in terms of developing trust and goodwill between people. They are a bedrock for collegial and work relationships, just as they are for intimate ones.

A FINAL WORD

Harmony at Home is the seventh and final character trait to prompt Unrelenting Drive, Dedication, and Determination. Imagine a person embodying, along with this trait, Unconditional Personal Responsibility, Passionate Purpose, Fearlessness, Interpersonal Intelligence, Mental Muscle, and Robust Vitality.

This person would be unstoppable. He or she would be extraordinarily well positioned to create great results, however he or she personally defined them.

NOTE

1   If it is possible to plagiarize from oneself, I plead guilty. In this chapter, I have drawn deeply, sometimes word for word, from another of my books, *The Couples Therapy Companion: A Cognitive Behavior Workbook,* published in 2015 by Routledge. If the ideas shared herein spark an interest in deepening your relationship harmony and happiness, for whatever reason, I direct you with enthusiasm to that book.

REFERENCES AND SUGGESTED READING

Chapman, G. (1995). *The five love languages: How to express heartfelt commitment to your mate.* Chicago, IL: Northfield Publishing.

Grieger, R. (2015). *The couples therapy companion: A cognitive behavior workbook.* New York: Routledge.

Hauck, P. A. (1994). *The three faces of love.* Philadelphia, PA: Westminster.

Kubie, L. S. (1956). "Psychoanalysis and marriage: Practical and theoretically issues." In V.W. Einstein (Ed.). *Neurotic interaction in marriage.* New York: Basic Books.

Maalouf, J. (2001). *Mother Theresa: essential writings.* Mary Knoll, NY: Orbis Books.

CHAPTER 9

Epilogue

Going forward with gusto

For there to be anything of greatness there must be a long obedience in the same direction.
Friedrich Nietzsche

In this book, I have asserted that each of us has within us the wherewithal to produce greatness in our lives, however we define it. Yes, each and every one of us, no exception allowed or permitted.

Greatness, to be sure, need not be a public or even an earth-shattering thing, such as what Albert Einstein, Wolfgang Amadeus Mozart, or Thomas Jefferson accomplished. No, greatness can be something quite personal, accomplished in private, within the confines of our own corner of the universe, such as the greatness my mother, Florence Grieger, produced within her family.

Fortunately, we are not left to wonder what it takes to achieve great results. Through a wide array of research across multiple fields, not to mention scores upon scores of human examples, we know that greatness requires three primary ingredients, all linked together into a dynamic, synergistic whole. They are:

1. hard, sustained effort, supported by . . .
2. vibrant, palpable dedication and determination, fueled by . . .
3. unrelenting drive, emanating from seven deep character traits, as follows:

   (1) Unconditional Personal Responsibility
   (2) Passionate Purpose
   (3) Fearlessness
   (4) Interpersonal Intelligence
   (5) Mental Muscle
   (6) Robust Vitality
   (7) Harmony at Home.

Each of these seven traits is learnable, growable, and sustainable. In Chapters 2 through 8, I described exactly what these traits are, provided workshops to assess the degree to which the reader possesses them and guide the reader to devise a workable action plan to develop each trait, and explained additional strategies to intensify them. I am confident anyone can succeed in growing each of these, but only if they choose to follow through on their action plan, as I (imperfectly, I might add) and innumerable others have done.

Please do not make the mistake of thinking that a person can internalize these traits simply by understanding them. The truth is that one needs to work at integrating them into one's thinking and behavior patterns, hence the importance of the workshops in each of these chapters.

A BEGINNING, NOT AN END

Before I conclude this book, I want to share the following three mindsets. If embraced, they can empower anyone to view his or her character growth and the pursuit of greatness as a fervent, life-long journey. They are: enlightened self-responsibility; freedom; and proactive commitment.

Enlightened Self-Responsibility

When we were of tender age, our parents had the responsibility of taking care of us. Being virtually helpless, it was their duty to ensure our physical survival, our emotional well-being, and our characterological development. After all, since they brought us into the world without our say-so, they had an ethical and legal job to prepare us to live independently once we reached the age of emancipation.

After this initial period in which our parents hopefully prepped us to succeed in life, it became our job. The adoption of three perspectives can empower us to take hold of the reins of our life and relentlessly strive to produce our great results:

1. In the midst of an indifferent universe, *no one – absolutely no one – is put on this earth to take care of us, to make our life work, or to see to it that we achieve our goals. It is our responsibility.* We, and no one else, are 100% responsible for the content and quality of our life: how we think and act, the way we deal with adversity, and what we do and do not achieve. It is entirely up to us.

2. While some would argue that there is a benevolent, all-powerful God who has a special purpose and plan for each of us, the fact of the matter is that it is objectively impossible to know whether or not there is an intrinsic meaning to our life or even a purpose to life at all. What we do know is that *we are here, and it is up to us to determine our life's purpose.* Perhaps the safest and possibly most empowering conclusion to draw is that only by living this life fully engaged – with purpose, vibrancy, and passion – does our life make sense.

3. We are all, as Martin Heidegger tells us, "Being-unto-Death" (Heidegger, 1962). *Our steady journey to death is a necessary fact about our existence, and sooner or later, at some future point in time, we will not exist*, at least in our present consciousness. Staring this sobering fact in the face forces us to take one of two paths: (1) ignore this destination, refuse to take our life seriously, and live in a state of passive reactivity; or (2) embrace the fact of our death and proactively choose to take hold of the direction and content of our life.

Freedom

The above realizations may not strike you as very cheerful or helpful. The fact that we are 100% responsible for our lives, that there may be no intrinsic meaning to life, and that sooner or later we will not exist might even sound bleak and depressing.

Yet, if you think about it, these perspectives are exceedingly liberating. For they free us, even goad us, to create our own life's purpose, to direct our life to what is personally meaningful and significant, to create our own best existence. How we live and what we define as greatness becomes our own personal choice. We are indeed free to create our life as we want.

Perhaps we would all be wise to envision ourselves on our deathbed. Imagine laying there asking ourselves these questions: Did I live a life of meaning? Did I take significant advantage of my time? Was my life one that meant something? If the bald, stark answer is an emphatic "No," or even a semi-waffling "Kind of," we'd be wise to ask: What could I now do to answer a resounding "Yes" to these questions? Then swing immediately into action.

With this freedom, and thus the self-responsibility accompanying it, we are not without tools. It is our good fortune to be blessed with a mind like no other in the universe, as far as we know – one capable of abstract thought, and with at least three powerful attributes that can be used to our advantage if we choose to do so:

1. We have the *capacity for rational thought*. We can reflect on ourselves – our characteristics and traits, our thoughts, and our behaviors – just as we can on any other objects in the universe. We can anticipate the consequences of our actions and thereby adjust our behaviors accordingly. We can choose fact over fiction, reason over bigotry, and right over wrong. Though the capacity for rational thought requires effort and intention, it provides the freedom to choose what is in our best interests.

2. We have the *capacity to envision* the possibilities for our future. Though we are sometimes burdened by the harsh facts of our innate limitations,

as well as the brute realities of our external circumstances, our visioning provides us with the option to act in ways to heighten the likelihood that these possibilities become realized.

3. We have the *capacity of conscience*. By "conscience," I mean the ability to evaluate how well we are living by social standards, moral and ethical codes, and our own ideal self-image. We can at any given moment ask whether or not we are being all we can be and make personal adjustments as necessary.

Proactive Commitment

Once we assume full, no-holds-barred responsibility for our life and freely determine both our life's purpose and our great goals, our proactive commitment to realize these drives relentless action. Be careful, though, not to view proactive commitment as an emotional thing comprised of enthusiasm, being fired up, or motivation, as these states wax and wane. Rather, proactive commitment represents a mentality characterized by these three principles:

1. *One lives by one's commitments*, as opposed to one's feelings, comfort, or convenience. It is a commitment to honor our commitments as the highest value; in other words, honoring our commitments becomes our highest ethic, such that, once we commit to an action or outcome, we act to honor the commitment despite any and all adverse circumstances.

2. *Authenticity becomes a primary virtue.* "Authenticity" means that, even with the acknowledgment of our history and circumstances, we take hold of our life by fully comporting ourselves according to our values and commitments.

3. *One rejects excuses.* Whatever the situation, one accepts that one is absolutely free and has choice. We are ultimately responsible for what we do, who we are, and what we achieve. There is a conscious decision to not waste time with excuse-making when thwarted, but instead to continue to live authentically, fully focused on doing what's necessary to achieve cherished results.

Please add these three philosophic elements to your Unrelenting Drive, Dedication, and Determination toolbox. Along with Unconditional Personal Responsibility, Passionate Purpose, Fearlessness, Interpersonal Intelligence, Mental Muscle, Robust Vitality, and Harmony at Home, these mindsets can further empower you to achieve the greatness in life you want. They add up to personal freedom, hope, and power – over yourself and your results.

A FINAL WORD

I want you to know how honored and privileged I am to have had the opportunity to communicate with you through the book. It has been an absolute pleasure to put what you have read on paper, as well as to know that you may use the book's contents to enrich your life and make your greatness happen. Thank you so very much for the privilege.

My sense of responsibility to you, however, does not end with your use of this book, at least in my mind. I sincerely invite you to contact me at any time if you want to further pick my brain. You can e-mail me anytime, as often as you want.

Russell Grieger, PhD

grieger@cstone.net

www.unrelentingdrive.com

Finally, go for it. You absolutely can produce greatness in your life, however you define it. I have given you the tools. Now it's up to you. Godspeed!

REFERENCES AND SUGGESTED READING

Heidegger, M. (1962). *Being and time.* New York: Harper & Row.

Nietzsche, F. (1997). *Beyond good and evil: Prelude to a philosophy of the future.* Minneola, NY: Dover Publications.

Acknowledgments

The more light you allow within you,
the brighter the world you live in will be.
Shakti Gawain

No one except perhaps the greatest genius creates something from nothing. What you have found in this book has many authors. Some I have known personally, others only through their prestigious work. Among those whose wisdom I have absorbed have been Dale Carnegie, the self-help guru of the mid-twentieth century; Stephen Covey, the author of the seminal text *The 7 Habits of Highly Effective People*; Werner Erhard, the founder of EST; His Holiness the Dalai Lama, a spiritual leader who translates the profound into the practical; Don Miguel Ruiz, Toltec healer and preacher whose teachings are truly transformational; Tony Robbins, life coach extraordinaire who is both inspirational and life changing; and, above all, Dr. Albert Ellis, a mentor and colleague who redefined psychotherapy yesterday, today, and tomorrow, and of whom more will be said shortly. With immense gratitude, I salute both their wisdom and their courage for putting it out there for our everlasting benefit. Where I may have forgotten to give credit where credit is due, I do so now.

Within my personal sphere, there have been many people who, by virtue of simply being who they are, have helped groom me to the point where I could write this book. Without any awareness or intent, they helped sculpt the perspectives and principles upon which I conduct my life. I think of my ol' buddy from high school, Allen McCutchan; my good friends from St. Louis, Gil Beckemier and Bob Coughenuer; and my uber college compatriot, Gene Hahn. I also think of the friends who have blessed my days in my adult years, including (in no particular order) Hal Burbach, Fred Fralick, John Boyd, Michael Kaminski, Judy Krings, and Jim Rodman. I have to add to this list Gary Grieger, a very successful businessman, a family man par excellence, and a wonderful "little" brother. From them, I have learned the ins and outs of Unrelenting Drive, Dedication, and Determination and so much more. Hopefully I have given a little something of value to them in return.

I would be remiss if I did not give my undying appreciation and gratitude to five men who have, each in their own way, been models of Unrelenting

Drive, Dedication, and Determination. Foremost among them is my father, Russell Grieger, Sr. Through thousands of hours of devoted and patient teaching, coaching, and cheerleading, my dad freely trafficked in open, unabashed passion. Among so much more, he demonstrated over and over again the benefits of pursuing goals without restraint, fear, or self-consciousness. My dad's life was a showcase for forthright, sustained effort to make what he longed for a reality.

To the great American psychologist Dr. Albert Ellis, I owe more than I can say. Dr. Ellis, the originator of Rational Emotive Behavior Therapy, was a giant, the most significant mental health professional of the twentieth century. Through his voluminous writings, lectures, and clinical demonstrations, and not a little bit by his personal example, he showed me and millions of others how to pursue life with purpose, perspective, and determination. Perhaps more than anyone else, he illuminated for me that the royal road to success is paved with Fearlessness and Mental Muscle.

I will always be grateful to my college basketball coach, Arad McCutchan. Contrary to the stereotypical coach of today who dominates his players through power, intimidation, and control, Coach McCutchan was a true gentleman, one who led through integrity, a sense of perspective, and wisdom. While expecting team rules to be followed, he mentored we players with respect, an expectation that we should do our best within the limits of our natural abilities, and poise under pressure. He truly was a life coach whose legacy went beyond Xs and Os to hearts and souls: Unconditional Personal Responsibility, Interpersonal Intelligence, and Mental Muscle.

Dr. Paul Grabil came into my life at a most opportune time. Professor of English literature at the University of Evansville, he befriended me when a hearty bout of self-acceptance was needed. Both through the example of how he conducted himself while carrying the handicap of a debilitating physical condition, and through the perspectives on life he shared, Dr. Grabil taught me two of the most important life success lessons: one, passionately pursue your goals no matter what your circumstances; two, totally and unconditionally accept yourself no matter what.

I also give loving thanks to Bill Stocker. Being some 15 years older than me, Bill was more my big brother than the man who married my cousin Beverly. After retiring from the vice-presidency of a major American corporation, he went through a deep personal crisis only to emerge stronger and wiser than ever. More instructive to me than his success in the business world, which was considerable, was the serenity he achieved later in life through his devotion to helping others. He died peacefully in his sleep, a man satisfied he had made the very best he could with his life.

Above all, I am most indebted to my family. My sons Todd and Gabriel are everything I hoped and prayed they would be, and more. To my wife, Patti,

I owe the greatest debt of all. Gracing my life now for 30 years, she is a daily inspiration for Interpersonal Intelligence. She blesses me with a cocoon of affection, a safe haven to pursue my life's work, and a continuing source of affirmation. She combines the roles of partner, playmate, and friend into one delicious package.

REFERENCES AND SUGGESTED READING

Gawain, S. (1986). *Living in the light: A guide to personal and planetary transformation.* Novato, CA: Nataras Publishing.

About Russell Grieger

Russell Grieger leads a vibrant, engaged professional life. As a practicing clinical psychologist with over 35 years' experience, he has helped individuals, couples, and families overcome the roadblocks to leading rich, fulfilling lives. A world-recognized expert on Rational Emotive Behavior Therapy, he has written extensively on the application of these techniques to a wide variety of emotional problems.

Dr. Grieger has also consulted with individuals and groups at all levels of such organizations as manufacturing plants, retail stores, hotels and resorts, construction companies, government bodies, banks and other financial entities, educational institutions, social service agencies, health care facilities, and correctional institutions. In addition, he has authored and delivered hundreds of high-intensity training programs to a wide variety of business audiences, often through the Chamber of Commerce venue.

With the mission of helping organizations reach their potential for sustainable high performance, Dr. Grieger's highly interactive programs have included team building, managing change, leadership development, organizational communication, strategic planning, conflict resolution, and high-powered selling, among others. He has been a pioneer in developing methods to enhance an organization's culture of commitment, discipline, and personal responsibility, and also in teaching those in leadership roles how to garner the unbridled loyalty and cooperation from others needed for success.

Dr. Grieger is also an adjunct professor at the University of Virginia's School of Continuing and Professional Studies. In this role, he provides workshops and seminars in a wide variety of topics, all oriented toward professional and personal mastery.

Dr. Grieger received his undergraduate degree from the University of Evansville, where he played on two consecutive NCAA Championship-winning basketball teams, and his Masters and Doctoral degrees from the Ohio State University. He has authored eight professional books, over 50 chapters and articles, and a series of self-help audiocassettes, as well as co-edited a professional psychological journal. Most recently, he has completed a memoir about his college basketball team, the 1964–5 undefeated Evansville College NCAA champions, *The Perfect Season.*

A believer in a balanced life, Dr. Grieger is a steady practitioner of regular exercise, intellectual stimulation, and interpersonal closeness. He lives with his wife and son in Charlottesville, Virginia and spends frequent time on St. Thomas in the US Virgin Islands and the waters surrounding it.

Index